Six Strategies

THE

for Finding

LONELINESS

Real Connections

CURE

in Your Life

KORY FLOYD, PHD

Adamsmedia
Avon, Massachusetts

Published by
Adams Media, a division of F+W Media, Inc.
57 Littlefield Street, Avon, MA 02322. U.S.A.
www.adamsmedia.com

ISBN 10: 1-4405-8209-2
ISBN 13: 978-1-4405-8209-7
eISBN 10: 1-4405-8210-6
eISBN 13: 978-1-4405-8210-3

Printed in the United States of America.

10   9   8   7   6   5   4   3   2   1

Library of Congress Cataloging-in-Publication Data
Floyd, Kory.
The loneliness cure / Kory Floyd.
    pages cm
  ISBN 978-1-4405-8209-7 (pb) -- ISBN 1-4405-8209-2 (pb) -- ISBN 978-1-4405-8210-3
(ebook) -- ISBN 1-4405-8210-6 (ebook)
1. Loneliness. 2. Interpersonal relations. 3. Interpersonal communication. I. Title.
  BF575.L7F56 2015
  158.2--dc23
                        2015000812

This book is intended as general information only, and should not be used to diagnose or treat any health condition. In light of the complex, individual, and specific nature of health problems, this book is not intended to replace professional medical advice. The ideas, procedures, and suggestions in this book are intended to supplement, not replace, the advice of a trained medical professional. Consult your physician before adopting any of the suggestions in this book, as well as about any condition that may require diagnosis or medical attention. The author and publisher disclaim any liability arising directly or indirectly from the use of this book.

Example stories are true, but names and other details have been changed to protect confidentiality.

This publication is designed to provide accurate and authoritative information with regard to the subject matter covered. It is sold with the understanding that the publisher is not engaged in rendering legal, accounting, or other professional advice. If legal advice or other expert assistance is required, the services of a competent professional person should be sought.
—From a *Declaration of Principles* jointly adopted by a Committee of the American Bar Association and a Committee of Publishers and Associations

Many of the designations used by manufacturers and sellers to distinguish their products are claimed as trademarks. Where those designations appear in this book and F+W Media, Inc. was aware of a trademark claim, the designations have been printed with initial capital letters.

Cover design by Frank Rivera.

This book is available at quantity discounts for bulk purchases.
For information, please call 1-800-289-0963.

Contents

Acknowledgments

Writing a book is like leaving on an extended vacation with only the vaguest of itineraries. Although I know generally where I want to go, it takes patience, curiosity, and a sense of adventure to discover how to get there. And, along the way, I meet a variety of people who stop, listen, and point me in the right direction. Even though I'm driving, it is these folks who make the journey what it is.

First, I am grateful for all the people who have shared their stories and experiences of affection and affection hunger with me over the past two decades. Their lives are the heart and soul of this book, and I appreciate their willingness to share so that others may benefit.

My agent, Linda Konner, has been a superb tour guide. She took a rough idea and helped me—and others—see its potential. She is a trusted advisor and her support has been invaluable.

I am immensely grateful to my editor, Tom Hardej, for shepherding this book from first draft to final product. He has been a true partner in this endeavor, and I appreciate his insights and his support for my message. He was ably assisted by Laura Daly, my development editor; Frank Rivera, who designed the cover; and

Bethany Carland-Adams, who oversaw publicity. I thank each of them for their contributions.

My colleagues and students are a continual source of joy and encouragement, as are my many friends in the field of interpersonal communication. They challenge and sharpen my thinking, and their collective intellect keeps me humble. I am truly blessed to have such a strong collection of wonderful friends and colleagues, and I appreciate them every day.

My most profound gratitude goes to my family and my partner Brian. They are my everlasting source of affection, and I couldn't be more grateful.

"Brother, Can You Spare a Hug?"

They say one man can make a difference. Evidently, so can "Juan Mann." In January 2004, he left behind his life in London, England, and returned to his home in Sydney, Australia. It was a lonely time for the twenty-two-year-old bachelor. His parents had divorced, his grandmother had fallen ill, and he had recently ended a promising relationship with his fiancée. One night, feeling dejected and alone, he went to a party, hoping to cheer himself up. Sometime that evening, a complete stranger approached him and gave him a hug. That small gesture had a profound effect. "I felt like a king!" he recalls. "It was the greatest thing that ever happened."

His elation was far from fleeting. Six months later, still riding an emotional high from that gift of unexpected affection, he decided to pay his good fortune forward. He found himself in Pitt Street Mall, a bustling pedestrian-only shopping center in the heart of Sydney's business district. It was a Wednesday in late June, and there he stood amidst the shoppers and businesspeople, the sightseers and families, holding a cardboard sign on which he had inked a simple message: Free Hugs.

He admits to feeling terrified at first. Would anyone take him up on his offer? Would people find his proposition strange, creepy, even pathological? He'd stood on the street for fifteen minutes—what felt like an eternity—before an elderly woman approached. As they shared an embrace, these two strangers in the middle of a busy marketplace, a worldwide movement was born.

Ever since that hug at the party in January had lifted Juan's spirits so much, he'd been eager for a way to give back. "I used to say to my friends, 'I'm just one man. What can I do?'" he remembers. What he did was start the Free Hugs Campaign, a social movement that now stretches across Australia and New Zealand, Asia, Europe, the Middle East, Africa, the United States and Canada, and Latin America. Recalling that he'd wondered what *one man* could do, he adopted the pseudonym *Juan Mann* . . . and by 2006, he and his movement were famous. A video of his efforts, featuring music by the Australian rock band Sick Puppies, has been viewed more than 70 million times on YouTube. He's been on *Oprah*. Free-hug events have taken place in the most diverse of places, from Israel, Taiwan, and Uganda to India, Malta, and the Dominican Republic. Inspired by what Juan Mann could do, people everywhere seemed to be spreading the love. That includes the United States, where free huggers can be found from San Diego to Boston, Seattle to Boca Raton.

By all accounts, the movement couldn't have reached U.S. shores at a better time. As a group, we Americans are starved for affection.

Perhaps you can identify with Juan Mann. How often do you find yourself feeling lonely, or craving more affection than you get? Maybe you wish your spouse or partner were a bit more expressive, or maybe you've tried without success to get certain people in your life to be more affectionate with you, so you go on wishing and hoping for more affection than you get. If these descriptions sound familiar, you're experiencing a common problem known as *affection hunger*. And you're not alone.

How widespread is the problem? Consider the following:

- More Americans than ever—nearly 28 percent—are living alone
- One in four Americans reports having not a single person to talk to about important issues
- Loneliness among American adults has increased by 15 percent just in the last decade
- Three of every four American adults agree that Americans are affection deprived
- We touch our cell phones more than we touch each other

These findings paint a picture of a people experiencing affection hunger, meaning they don't get as much affection as they need and they hunger for more quality human interaction. We normally associate hunger with food, of course—but we don't feel hungry simply because we *want* food. We feel hungry because we *need* food, just as we feel thirsty because we need water and tired because we need sleep. Our bodies know what they require to function properly, and as I'll explain in this book, meaningful human contact belongs on that list right next to food, water, and rest.

Meaningful is the key word. The truth is, if you have hundreds of acquaintances but you don't feel close to any of them—close enough that you give and receive affection with them—you can still feel lonely. Your loneliness might be situational, if, for example, the stress of a major deadline at work keeps you from sharing quality time with your spouse and children. Loneliness can also be chronic, wherein you constantly long for more substantial contact from those you know and love. Either way, loneliness, and its ensuing hunger for affection, is a condition that many people experience. *If you feel lonely, you likely aren't receiving the amount of affectionate human contact that you desire. And, as I'll show you in this book, affection is absolutely vital to your mental and physical well-being.*

Maybe that's why the Free Hugs Campaign struck such a nerve. There's now an International Free Hug Day celebrated in early July each year, as well as a Collegiate International Free Hug Day that has its own app. Whatever his real name is, Juan Mann must have a satisfied smile on his face to see his movement proliferate the way it has.

To be sure, sharing more affection with other people isn't going to end poverty or solve the U.S. unemployment problem. Hugging more won't free us from dependence on foreign oil or eradicate world hunger. That doesn't mean your need for affection is trivial, though. Relationships that offer opportunities to give and receive affection *can* solidify and strengthen your connection to the world around you, increase your sense of optimism and fortitude, counteract depression, and improve your body's abilities to manage stress.

In other words, it won't solve our global problems, but it will better equip us to. This book will be a first step toward easing loneliness in your own life. In this book, I will:

- Explain what it means to hunger for social connections and affection
- Illustrate how common and widespread the problem is
- Describe the causes behind affection hunger and the problems associated with it
- Help you assess your own needs for human connection
- Offer six compelling strategies for attracting more genuine connection in your life

Maybe you've wondered how you can get your husband or your girlfriend to be more affectionate with you. Perhaps you'd like to take your relationship with a friend to the next level. If those situations sound familiar, then you already understand what affection hunger is. I can't recall when I first heard the term *affection hunger*, but it was one of those beautiful moments when you discover the perfect name for an idea. If you find yourself hungry for more relationships that include affection, you probably realize as well what an apt description it is.

In the two decades I have spent studying affection, the one question I've been asked more than any other is "How can I get more?" I understand that need, and this book will show you how.

How to Use This Book

If you want more affection and less loneliness in your life, I'm inviting you to take a journey with me in this book. Pack lightly, because we have much to pick up along the way.

We're going to begin our voyage by reflecting a bit on your experiences, your expectations, and your common patterns of behavior. To decide where you're going, it's first necessary to figure out where you are. Once we know that a little better, we will explore how you are similar to, and different from, other people in terms of how you communicate your affection in relationships and the benefits you can expect from addressing your affection hunger.

As we proceed on our trip, we'll stop and acknowledge a variety of behaviors people use to communicate affection. These behaviors are an important part of making and maintaining quality relationships, and combatting loneliness in the process. During this portion of our voyage, you may encounter ways of expressing affection that were previously unfamiliar to you, so it will help if you can keep an open mind.

The rockiest part of our journey awaits us when we survey some of the most common mistakes people make when trying to increase social connections and affection in their lives. These mistakes result from misunderstanding what leads to loneliness and affection hunger in the first place. It's as if your doctor didn't realize that your cold was caused by a virus, so he treated it with an antibiotic, a topical skin cream, or an antidepressant. Those treatments would be ineffective because none of them addresses the actual problem—and the same is true for the mistakes people commonly make regarding affection. Sadly, people who continue to feel affection deprived over time tend to cope with that feeling in some unconstructive ways, as we'll explore.

Finally, after travailing, we reach our destination: an examination of effective strategies for combatting loneliness and meeting your affection needs. If you're considering this journey at all, you've probably felt the frustration of experiencing affection hunger and attempting without success to improve your situation. Many people eventually come to believe their loneliness is a permanent state, when in fact, they simply haven't learned how to address it successfully. The answers are there, though, if we know where to find them. That's the purpose of our travels in this book.

Welcome aboard—I'm glad to have you along on this trip.

PART ONE

Why Do People Need Social Connection?

Our journey to alleviate loneliness begins in Part One, where we will discover why people are affectionate in the first place. Chapter One, Hungry for Connection, describes how we need affection in our lives in order to thrive, and why our desire for social connection is so strong that we hunger for affection when we don't get enough. In Chapter Two, Why We Love, we explore the connections between love and survival. We also learn how affectionate behavior evolved and why it is beneficial only under certain conditions. Finally, Chapter Three, How Affection Helps, explains the benefits of affection for mental and physical health and illustrates the many links between social disconnection and stress.

CHAPTER ONE

Hungry for Connection

Cara rocks quietly in her chair as she glances at the clock on her nightstand. 2:36 A.M. Barely an hour ago, her small home was filled with the noises of a cranky and resolutely unsettled three-week-old. Now, a satisfying stillness hangs in the air as Cara holds her baby Jacob, wrapped in a warm flannel blanket, against her chest. On the bed next to them, her husband Matt lies sleeping on his side, facing Cara and their son. Although she is tired, Cara is not sleepy. Rather, in this moment, she is calm, relishing her peace and safety while sitting between the two most important men in her life. At the same time, as she looks at Jacob and hears him breathe, as she smells his skin and feels his warmth against hers, she is overwhelmed with how all-consuming her love is for him. In some small place in her mind, she even wonders whether she loves Jacob more than she loves Matt, because she has never experienced affection this deep and compelling before. She draws her son closer with one arm as she rubs her husband's shoulder with her other hand, and she asks herself silently if she has ever, in her entire twenty-four years, felt this loved.

Cara wouldn't necessarily realize it, but she craves the tender warmth of little Jacob and the unselfish love of her husband Matt for reasons that are entirely primal. In so doing, she awakens once again a primitive drive that burned deep in her own mother's heart, and that of her mother's mother, and her grandmother's mother, and so forth, back thousands of generations. In this moment, here in the quiet and stillness of the night, with Jacob wrapped softly next to her bosom, Cara really doesn't need to realize the primal roots of her feelings. Of this she is certain, however: She not only *wants* this love that she feels washing over her. She *needs* it.

And that's precisely what connects her to all the women—indeed, all the people—who precede her on her family tree. Perhaps you've felt that way, too, in those instances when you realize that love and affection are more than just luxuries that make you feel happy and secure. They are, instead, parts of our experience that we could no more do without than the air we breathe or the water we drink. Maybe you don't recognize how valuable those resources are to you when you have them in abundance. Cut off your oxygen supply, though, and you'll quickly appreciate the difference between a luxury and a requirement.

Did You Know?

Loneliness is bad for your health. According to research, lonely adults consume more fat, drink more alcohol, get less exercise, and sleep less soundly than people who aren't lonely.

We can't live without oxygen, and it turns out that we can't live without affection, either. *Along with food, water, air, and sleep, we need affection to survive.* Perhaps that sounds like an exaggeration, and if it does, I can understand why. I would likely have said the same before I started studying love, human connection, and affection. Now, though, the collective results of hundreds of studies—my own and those of other social scientists—have thoroughly convinced me otherwise. Just as we can be starved for oxygen or food, we can be starved for affection, and the physical, mental, and psychological effects can be ruinous. It's a fundamental biological need, one that we cannot afford to ignore—so when Cara finds her heart stirred by the depth of love surrounding her, she is moved by the satisfaction of a basic life requirement that has been with our species for millennia.

And today, unfortunately, thousands of us are starving to meet that need in our own lives.

A State of Disconnection

Jennifer's Story

AFTER TWENTY-EIGHT YEARS, JENNIFER'S MARRIAGE TO HER HUSBAND ELLIOTT WAS FEELING STALE. "HE WAS REALLY ROMANTIC WHEN WE FIRST GOT TOGETHER," SHE RECALLS. "HE USED TO LEAVE ME LOVE NOTES ON THE MIRROR IN OUR BATHROOM, AND HE'D BRING HOME BIG BUNCHES OF TULIPS BECAUSE HE KNOWS THAT'S MY FAVORITE FLOWER." NOW, HOWEVER, IT FEELS LIKE THEY'RE BOTH JUST GOING THROUGH THE MOTIONS. THEY RARELY SAY *I LOVE YOU* TO EACH OTHER, AND THEIR SEX IS ROUTINE AND UNSATISFYING. JENNIFER UNDERSTANDS THAT THIS IS NOT UNCOMMON AFTER SO MANY YEARS TOGETHER, BUT IT LEAVES HER CONSTANTLY WANTING MORE AFFECTION THAN SHE GETS.

Many of us find ourselves in a condition I call *affection hunger*, which simply means we want more affection from other people than we receive. Affection usually grows out of meaningful social connections, so if you're hungry for affection, you probably feel lonely as well. If you can relate to that feeling, maybe you wish you had more friends you could talk to about important matters. Or perhaps you want someone specific to be more outwardly affectionate with you, such as your husband or wife, your boyfriend or girlfriend, your dad or your daughter. That's how Jennifer feels with her husband Elliott. Or, maybe you wish for more affectionate connections from other people in general. Whatever your situation, you probably know what I mean when I use the term "affection hunger" to describe that feeling. If so, then you might not be surprised to learn that our hunger for affection has some things in common with regular, everyday hunger.

We Hunger for Affection

It may not seem so, but nature did us a solid by creating the sensation we call hunger. To survive, each of our bodies needs access to a minimum number of calories per day, on average. Like water and oxygen, food is a necessity, not a luxury. If we were to stop eating altogether, of course, we'd first experience malnutrition and eventually reach starvation, the point at which our bodies have exhausted all available sources of energy and we are on the brink of death. The necessity of eating regularly, therefore, is something we can't afford to forget. Fortunately, nature didn't entrust that task to our fallible memories. Instead, it gave us a built-in reminder: hunger.

Those discomforting feelings we call hunger pangs come to us courtesy of two hormones, leptin and ghrelin. Leptin gets triggered when we eat and is responsible for making us feel full. Our leptin levels drop several hours after a meal, stimulating the release of ghrelin. High levels of ghrelin coupled with low levels of leptin get our tummies rumbling. That's when we experience hunger, that unpleasant state that motivates us to find food. It doesn't matter whether we eat a light snack or gorge ourselves on a Thanksgiving feast—we can count on our hunger returning every few hours, day in and day out, reminding us to eat.

Hunger, in other words, is nature's way of making sure we get enough of something we need to survive. It's our caloric wake-up call, and if we ignore it—either on purpose or involuntarily—we experience a range of health complications.

We can make similar observations about our hunger for affection:

- Like regular hunger, it is connected to something we need for survival: intimate human contact.
- Like regular hunger, it feels bad when we experience it and good when we satisfy it.
- It leads to health complications and prompts undesirable compensatory behaviors when it's ignored.
- Like depriving prisoners of food, depriving them of social contact—in the form of solitary confinement—is, even today, considered to be among the harshest of punishments.

The Emptiness of Modern Connections

What's challenging about our hunger for affection is that it's so much easier to ignore than regular hunger. That's because most of us live our daily lives surrounded by other people, either in real or virtual form. We live, work, go to school, do our grocery shopping, eat, see movies and concerts, worship, volunteer, and exercise in various social communities. And wherever we turn these days, we see examples of the world getting smaller around us. You can go online and, within moments, be chatting in real time with someone on a different continent. I can press a few keys on my smartphone and cause a text message to appear on my sister's phone 3,000 miles away. Over Skype, deployed servicemen can witness the birth of their children in hospitals back home, *almost as if they were there in person.* Celebrities, politicians, and even the British royals have their own Facebook pages and regularly post YouTube videos. Some famous people have thousands (or hundreds of thousands) of followers on Twitter who are privy to every thought and opinion and complaint they choose to tweet. (Justin Bieber currently has more than 57 million Twitter followers, although controversies rage in the blogosphere over whether his marketing sharks inflate that number so as to stay ahead of chief rival Lady Gaga. Stay tuned.) Those technologies allow us to hear from famous people so often—and learn so much about them—that we feel as though we *know* them.

Andrew's Story

ANDREW'S GIRLFRIEND JANAE GETS UPSET WHEN THEY'RE SPENDING TIME TOGETHER AND HE HAS TO TAKE A CALL ON HIS CELL PHONE. SHE FEELS HE'S CHOOSING HIS CELL PHONE OVER HER, WHICH ANDREW THINKS IS RIDICULOUS. AFTER TWO YEARS OF BEING TOGETHER, HE BELIEVES SHE SHOULD UNDERSTAND THAT HE SOMETIMES GETS IMPORTANT CALLS FROM WORK THAT HE NEEDS TO ANSWER. WHAT HE MAY NOT REALIZE IS THAT JANAE FEELS LIKE SHE'S COMPETING WITH HIS CELL PHONE FOR HIS ATTENTION . . . AND LOSING. AFTER AN HONEST DISCUSSION ABOUT THE PROBLEM, ANDREW AGREED TO LET JANAE KNOW AHEAD OF TIME IF HE'S EXPECTING AN IMPORTANT CALL. OR, IF AN URGENT CALL COMES IN, HE AGREED TO TELL HER IT'S IMPORTANT BEFORE ANSWERING IT. BECAUSE OF THEIR OPEN COMMUNICATION, JANAE NO LONGER FEELS OVERLOOKED WHEN ANDREW MUST ANSWER HIS PHONE, AND ANDREW IS MORE CONSIDERATE ABOUT THE EFFECTS OF HIS ACTIONS ON HER FEELINGS.

The Internet makes commonplace what previous generations could scarcely have envisioned: communication at an individual level, in real time, with anyone who can get online anywhere. Just think for a moment about all the different ways someone can get in touch with you. If you're like many people, you can be reached by cell phone or land line, by e-mail (on how many different accounts? The average American has more than three), on your Facebook wall or Twitter, on other social networking sites (such as LinkedIn or Foursquare), by Skype, by text message, by snail mail, and of course, by an actual face-to-face visit.

Did You Know?

The mere presence of a cell phone reduces closeness. According to research, just having a mobile device visible during a conversation makes people feel less close and connected, even if the device never rings.

Few of us are ever more than a call, click, text, or tweet away from anyone else in our lives, and that expansive capacity to communicate supports the comforting illusion that we're more connected to each other than ever before. What we so often ignore, however, is the emotional depth—or the lack thereof—of those techno-interactions we have at our continual disposal. We can share the most mundane information about our lives through the 140 characters a Twitter message affords, but often feel inhibited about offering something beyond the superficial. As a result, we end up glorifying the trivial ("I JUST GOT BIEBER TICKETS!!!") while barely noticing that the substantive and meaningful are missing.

Our Efforts Create Pseudo-Intimacy

To many, what ends up mattering instead is a type of pseudo-intimacy, a condition bearing the sheen of true human attachment but without the effort it takes to nurture or the sacrifice it requires to maintain. That's a fitting description for the Japanese man who, in 2009, held a wedding ceremony in which he married one of the characters from the Nintendo DS video game Love Plus. The young man, whose screen name is "Sal9000," became hooked on the 2-D game in which players aim to court young cyber-darlings in an attempt to win their love. In the game, total devotion is rewarded with a deeper relationship, and Sal9000 became wholly devoted to Nene Anegasaki, his Love Plus honey. Their wedding ceremony was broadcast live on the Internet. One can only be grateful they didn't show the honeymoon.

Another example is Cloud Girlfriend, a website that allows users to "friend" a fake girlfriend on Facebook. Users receive messages on their wall from the profile of a counterfeit sweetheart. Cofounder David Fuhriman thinks that sporting a faux girlfriend will help guys attract the real thing. As the company's website boasts, "The best way to get a girlfriend is to already have one."

In other words, Cloud Girlfriend is the twenty-first-century equivalent of sending yourself candy and flowers. The motive behind both activities is to appear desired and, therefore, desirable. Perhaps you're mature enough to be above such nonsense . . . but do you ever compare how many Facebook friends you have to how many other people have? If so, then you, too, engage in the entirely human activity of social comparison. That's when we perceive our own social standing by comparing ourselves to others. I might think of myself as popular if I have 300 Facebook friends and most people I know have fewer than 100. When I start noticing people with upwards of 700 friends, though, suddenly I don't feel so popular anymore. Nothing about my own situation has changed—I still have the same number of friends as before—but my *perception of myself* has changed due to social comparison. In the same vein, if I have a beautiful woman posting love notes on my Facebook wall—even if I'm paying a service to make that happen (we can call that cyber-hooking)—I feel more popular and desirable and socially successful than others.

That sense of popularity can be dangerously like *The Wizard of Oz*'s man behind the curtain, though. Of what comfort are my 300 Facebook friends if I still feel fundamentally alone in the world? They're there to reach out to, yes. I can poke them or IM them or post on their wall, but at some point those activities cease to resemble meaningful communication. A tweet or text is easily ignored, like so much cyber–junk mail, requiring no real engagement of my heart or mind. That's why we can be bombarded with words on a daily basis and still feel so alone. The sheer volume of interaction we have with others masks a troubling reality: *Even as the* quantity *of our connections with other people is on the rise, the* quality *of our connections is often taking a turn for the worse.* We know more people, but we know them less. We have more friends, but we're less trustful of them. Our world is more social than ever, yet we feel more alone than at any time in our modern history.

Why We Need Social Connection

Once grown up, the Bornean orangutan (*Pongo pygmaeus*) looks a bit like a ginger-haired gorilla whose face got smashed by a frying pan. Native to Southeast Asia, this primate spends its first several years of life eating, sleeping, and traveling with its mother. It's a powerful bond. Says scientist and conservationist Dr. Biruté Mary Galdikas, "Only humans have a more intensive relationship with their mothers. Primatologists believe that orangutans have such long 'childhoods' because there is so much that they need to learn before they can live alone successfully." During that time, adolescents learn to forage for wild figs, bird eggs, seeds, insects, and fish. They discover how to bend and weave small branches to build arboreal nests just before sunset each night. They learn to use sticks to knock down fruit from trees, and leaves to wipe themselves clean. In short: all the lessons necessary for modern orangutan living.

As soon as those formative years are complete, though, the Bornean orangutan lives most of its remaining life alone. Aside from an occasional mating tryst in the shrubbery, females spend time with other orangutans only when rearing their offspring— and males, only when defending their territories. Beyond those necessary tasks, orangutans don't invest much time or attention in each other. They've got stuff to do. Plus, it's not in their nature: The Bornean orangutan is perhaps the most solitary of all the primates. It isn't that they couldn't develop a rich social life if they wanted to . . . they simply aren't programmed for that.

We humans share 97 percent of our DNA with the Bornean orangutan. Let that fact germinate in your mind for a moment. DNA—*deoxyribonucleic acid*—provides the genetic blueprint for building a living organism, whether it's a jellyfish, a chanterelle mushroom, an Asian cockroach, a wedge-tailed eagle, or a person. Only 3 percent of the instructions for building a Bornean orangutan are different from the instructions for building a human being. We could hardly share more of our DNA with another species and still *be* a separate species. Only to chimps and gorillas are we more closely related genetically.

Despite our striking genetic similarity with the Bornean orangutan, however, we couldn't be more different when it comes to our social needs. *Homo sapiens* is easily the *least* solitary of all the primates. To put it differently, humans have a pressing, overwhelming drive to be social.

We Need to Belong

In his 2006 book, *Personal Relationships and Personal Networks*, interpersonal communication scholar Malcolm Parks writes, "We humans are social animals down to our very cells. Nature did not make us noble loners." He's right. We don't spend our lives like the Bornean orangutan, wandering the world in solitary bliss. We bond to each other. We work and play and live in communities, some as small as a marriage and some as large as a country. We rely on others—whether our next-door neighbors or the United Nations—to help us in times of crisis, and we offer our own help, even to strangers, when we perceive a need. We identify with our relationships in outward ways, such as by wearing wedding rings or taking a new spouse's last name, and in inward ways, such as by thinking of "us" rather than "you and me." We display our allegiance to our country, our sports teams, our political parties, our religions, and our alma maters with fervor and pride. Almost nothing we do as humans doesn't feed our affection hunger in one way or another—we even prefer to sleep next to the ones we love.

Why do we invest in social connections at every turn while our primate cousins meander contentedly in isolation? Psychologist Roy Baumeister believes it's because humans have a fundamental drive to form and nurture meaningful interpersonal bonds that he calls the *need to belong*. Along with fellow psychologist Mark Leary, Baumeister has argued that the need to belong is an innate motivation—not one we learn but one we're born with—that characterizes all people, regardless of their cultural, economic, religious, or ethnic backgrounds. Everyone needs to belong, according to Professors Baumeister and Leary.

Allen's Story

ALLEN STARTED FEELING LONELY NOT LONG AFTER HE STARTED COLLEGE. EVEN THOUGH HE LIVED IN A FRATERNITY HOUSE AND WAS USUALLY SURROUNDED BY PEOPLE, HE DIDN'T HAVE ANYONE HE COULD REALLY TALK TO. HE HAD A FEW SHORT-LIVED RELATIONSHIPS WITH WOMEN, BUT NEVER FOUND ANYBODY HE TRULY CONNECTED WITH. AS COLLEGE WENT ON, HIS LONELINESS GREW INTO MILD DEPRESSION. TO COMBAT HIS FEELINGS, HE STARTED HAVING SEXUAL HOOKUPS WITH STRANGERS HE MET ON CRAIGSLIST. AT ONE POINT, HE WAS HOOKING UP WITH SOMEONE ALMOST EVERY NIGHT. EVEN THOUGH HE ENJOYED THE PHYSICAL INTIMACY OF HIS ENCOUNTERS, HE STILL FELT AS LONELY AS EVER, NO MATTER HOW MANY PEOPLE HE HAD SEX WITH. IN OTHER WORDS, HIS FORAYS INTO PSEUDO-INTIMACY WERE CLEARLY NOT FULFILLING HIS HUNGER FOR REAL AFFECTION.

The Physical Implications of Belonging

Central to Baumeister and Leary's theory is the argument that satisfying our need to belong benefits us, whereas failing to meet it harms us. In the social sciences, few notions can claim more compelling support. On average, people with strong marriages and friendships are healthier, happier, and likely to live longer than those without. Being sociable, agreeable, and affectionate is associated with lower stress, a stronger immune system, and even a greater ability to ward off the common cold.

On the other hand, chronic loneliness is a recipe for disaster. Experiencing—or even just fearing—ostracism and social exclusion compromises the body's resistance to illness and ability to recover from injury. It dampens our capability for thought, exacerbates our depression, and is even considered a prime risk factor for suicide. After reviewing more than sixty published studies on the health implications of social ties, sociologist James House found that lacking strong, positive relationships elevates a person's risk of premature death as much as being obese, having high blood pressure, or smoking cigarettes.

Importantly, however, Baumeister and Leary point out that satisfying our need to belong requires interactions that are both *frequent* and *meaningful*. It's not enough to have a meaningful bond with someone you never get to see. Many people have such relationships, of course, especially if their partners are serving on military deployments or working away from home—but these ties don't really fulfill their need to belong, according to Baumeister and Leary. Moreover, it's not enough to have frequent interactions that are devoid of meaning, as Allen discovered. His hookups were sexually satisfying, but they did nothing to reduce his loneliness in the long term. Even physically intimate exchanges are inadequate to meet our need to belong if they aren't emotionally meaningful.

Our Need for Connection Begins Early

Our need for close relationships starts on the first day of our lives. Understanding what I mean by that requires us to think back enormously far, before humans resembled the species we recognize today. Many moons ago—somewhere between 3 and 6 million years in the past—our prehistoric ancestors took their first steps as bipedal beings (those who walk upright on two feet). This was before the emergence of *Homo sapiens*, the species to which we modern humans belong. Being able to walk on two feet offered many advantages to our ancestors—and, as you'd probably agree, it continues to be a good deal for us.

As with most developments, there are tradeoffs, and one in particular is relevant here. Being bipedal is greatly facilitated by having a narrow pelvis, which makes movement efficient and makes the pelvis less likely to break. The substantial tradeoff to having a narrow pelvis, though, is that it makes giving birth physically risky to both mother and child. Nature provides several accommodations, such as making the infant's skull pliable enough to pass through the birth canal and allowing the ligaments that hold together the mother's pelvic bones to relax during delivery. The most significant accommodation, though, is that to pass through the narrow female pelvis, human babies must be born in a state of considerable immaturity.

Consider, for comparison, most any of our cousins in the animal kingdom. A newborn giraffe, for instance, is walking and running behind its mother within hours of its birth. Mountain lion cubs learn to hunt for their own food at six months of age, and baby turtles are on their own from the moment their lives begin. We humans, in sharp contrast, enter this world in a condition of advanced dependency. Nature does not prepare us to fend for ourselves within hours, days, months, or even several years of our birth. Instead, each of us alive today relied wholly and completely on someone else to meet all our needs—shelter, food, clothing, protection, medical care, education, and so forth—for the first several years of our existence.

A human baby born today probably won't even begin walking for at least a year and may not truly fend for itself—that is, meet all of its own material needs—until well into adulthood. Up to then, your child depends on you. Every newborn's survival rests on somebody's willingness to provide for it.

Love Saves Our Lives

Because children, especially infants, can't fend for themselves, they rely on *conspecifics*—other members of their own species—to meet their needs. Let me pose what I mean to be a serious question: What motivates us to make such an extraordinary investment—financially, emotionally, and otherwise, over such a significant span of our own lives—in each of our kids? Why do we do that, willingly and on an ongoing basis? Although the question may strike you as absurd, consider that virtually none of us invests so much financially or emotionally in *other people's* children. Okay, our nieces and nephews, our grandchildren, the children of our closest friends—those we care about and will provide for when necessary. But when my child needs braces, I don't expect you to pay for them. I accept that as my responsibility, just as each of us does for our own children. Perhaps you'll drive the neighbor's kids to school or let them eat dinner at your house, but you're not planning to send them to college or help them get their first mortgages. They have their own parents for that.

Ask Yourself

In your life, whom do you give your significant resources (time, money, shelter) to?

So, we invest heavily in children, but only in *some* children—generally, our own and those who are related to us. But why do it at all?

The answer, of course, is that we love them—but here's an even trickier question: *Why* do we love them? Or, to make it slightly more concise, why do we love? The answer isn't as obvious as it should be. I know, because I've spent most of my career trying to understand it.

The Science of Affection

I have been interested in affection for a long time, both as an academic and as a human. It wouldn't be an exaggeration to say I grew up in a touchy-feely family. All of us—my dad, mom, sister, and brother—were pretty demonstrative. We hugged and kissed each other often. We shared *I love you*'s virtually every day. That may partly have been a function of living on the U.S. West Coast—which, along with the South, tends to be more touchy than the East or the Midwest, according to research. I attribute our family's affectionate personality more to my parents, though, who grew up in an era when children were to be seen and not heard and who were determined not to repeat that pattern with my siblings and me. Consequently, they instilled in us a healthy appreciation for the expression of our love for each other. And it helped, of course, that we actually *did* love each other.

Like most people, I carried the norms of my family with me into my interactions with others in the world. And like most people, I quickly discovered that what was normal to me wasn't normal to everyone. Since I had grown up associating *feelings of affection* with *expressions of affection*, I made it a point to let my social connections—classmates, teachers, and friends—know how much I cared about them. In high school, I got a reputation as a hugger, and it didn't faze me at all to tell my friends that I loved them.

Coming from a family like mine, I felt completely normal communicating with other people this way. But not everyone came from a family like mine.

Affection Can Be Tricky

During my high school and college years, I learned that expressing affection to others was, as often as not, an invitation to trouble. Many young women mistook my affection as a romantic gesture, which led invariably to confusion, sometimes to stalking, and occasionally to a drawn-out, tearful conversation in which I would come off looking insensitive, socially inept, or both. A few young men also mistook my affection as a romantic gesture, which usually prompted a period of avoidance followed by a man-to-man talk in which they, often defensively, would reveal that they didn't like me in "that way."

What I couldn't wrap my mind around, however, was that many people didn't know how to react to my affection at all. A few seemed genuinely put off by it, as though I'd insulted their religion and then asked them for money. To me, that was truly perplexing. How could something I meant so positively be received with indifference or even negativity? Doesn't everyone know how to show love, I wondered? That question eventually bugged me enough that I went to graduate school and studied the communication of affection for my PhD. (Years later, I remember hearing someone say the best researchers weren't driven as much by *curiosity* as by *confusion*, a point with which I heartily agreed.)

An important part of what I discovered is that many things get in the way of affection. Sometimes we don't want the affection we receive—because, perhaps, we're afraid of what it means for us or for our relationship. Even more often, though, we don't receive the affection we desire, because we succumb to social barricades that heighten our sense of isolation and contribute to our loneliness. For many, that creates a Catch-22: We don't get the affection we need, and as a result, we don't know how to respond to affection when we do get it.

Affection Comes in Many Forms

This conundrum is complicated by the fact that affection can take a wide range of forms, some of which can be easy to miss. When you hear people speak of love and affection, you may naturally think first about physical behaviors that are frequent in romantic relationships, such as kissing, holding hands, or having sex. You might also think of verbal messages, such as "I love you" or "I care about you." Each of these behaviors is common and important, yet our repertoire of affectionate expressions is actually much wider.

Among humans, affectionate behaviors come in three general forms:

- **Verbal:** Some affectionate expressions are verbal, which includes any message that is conveyed with words. "I love you," "you're important to me," and "I care for you" are all examples, whether spoken aloud, written in a card or text message, or even conveyed through sign language.

- **Nonverbal:** Other affectionate behaviors comprise what researchers call direct nonverbal gestures. These are behaviors that don't involve words but whose affectionate meaning is generally clear to those who receive them, such as hugging, kissing, and handholding.

- **Socially supportive:** Finally, some affectionate expressions take the form of socially supportive behaviors, which are actions that meet either an emotional or material need for the recipient. Acknowledging a coworker's birthday, listening to a sibling discuss a problem, and volunteering to help a friend move are all supportive behaviors that imply a level of care and affection for the receiver.

You may even have unique ways of showing affection that don't fit neatly into one of these three categories. The point is that we use a wide range of behaviors to convey messages of love, and this gives rise to two additional observations:

1. First, *affection is about more than romance.* Although most of us show affection to our romantic partners, we also do so with our families, our close friends, our neighbors, and anyone else for whom we have positive regard. Our behaviors may vary from person to person, but most of us give, receive, and value affection in a wide range of social connections.

2. Second, *affection can be easy to overlook.* As you saw, people sometimes communicate love by doing favors for us—and

although we might appreciate their help, we may not inter-pret it as an affectionate expression. Most of us wouldn't misunderstand the meaning of a hug or kiss, but we may overlook a message of care and affection that comes in the form of an empathic ear or a ride to the airport.

The Affection Lab

I've been writing, teaching, and thinking about these intrica-cies of affection for the last twenty years. At Arizona State University, where I currently work, my lab is officially called the Communication Sciences Laboratory but it might as well be called the Affection Lab. There, my graduate students and I study what affectionate behavior does to the body, and for the body. A welcomed hug can make you feel warm and relaxed, whereas receiving an unwelcomed hug might make you feel uncomfort-able or distressed—and in the Affection Lab, we try to understand why these reactions occur. What transpires inside the body to pro-duce those sensations? And if affectionate communication can bring a feeling of calm and alleviate stress, might it also have the benefit of combatting physical and mental health conditions that are exacerbated by stress? There are certainly many of those, from high cholesterol and blood pressure to depression, obesity, sleep-ing problems, even acne. Is it possible that helping people manage their stress better by sharing more affection with their loved ones could improve some of these health outcomes?

The answer is yes. Many of our scientific studies of affectionate behavior, as well as those done in other labs, have demonstrated its health benefits, and I'll describe some of those in this book. To me, understanding those benefits is a mixed blessing. I love knowing that sharing affection with my loved ones makes me feel good for a reason—because it is good *for me*. Nature saw to it that I crave that behavior for the same reasons I get hungry and thirsty and fatigued: In each case, it motivates me to seek something I require to sustain myself.

The flip side is that understanding the benefits of affection makes it all the more heartbreaking to know how many people aren't getting the level of social connection they need. I meet many adults who fit that category—perhaps you are one. Similarly, I worry about what some of our zero-tolerance, no-touch policies are doing to children, who need affection and connection every bit as much as we adults do. I worry about thirteen-year-old Megan Coulter, who was given detentions in 2007 from her Illinois middle school for hugging her friend on school grounds. I worry about eighth-grader Ryan Blackmon, suspended in 2012 from his Charlotte, North Carolina, middle school not for fighting, but for *hugging the teacher who broke up the fight.*

Did You Know?

Touch is essential for children's physical health. According to research, children who are touched grow faster, develop more fully, and have healthier immune responses than children who are touch deprived.

Is child sexual abuse a real concern? Of course, and no serious person would suggest otherwise. In responding to it, however, many of us have accepted an extreme baby-with-the-bathwater approach that not only defies reason but inadvertently introduces problems of its own, ones that I would argue are proportionally worse. I know we're trying to protect our kids, but what are we doing to them by denying them touch? Touch is an inherent part of showing love—a topic we'll explore in the next chapter.

Stop and Reflect

As you journey through this book, you'll find it useful to pause from time to time and think about how the discussion applies to you. To guide your self-reflection, I end each chapter with three questions. I encourage you to consider them carefully and answer them honestly. Write out your responses so you can reflect on how your perspective develops as you read. The more self-reflective you are, the better you will come to know yourself—and the better you know yourself, the more useful this book's strategies will be for you:

- Do you want more affection than you receive? How much more? Do you seek more affection from a specific person, or from people in general? What do you think keeps you from getting the level of affection you want?
- What types of social connections do you want to increase or strengthen in your life?
- How do you feel—both emotionally and physically—when you don't get the amount of affection you want?

CHAPTER TWO

Why We Love

No human experience has been pondered, pontificated about, or philosophized over more than love. Love is the single most common focus across genres of artistic creation—poetry, prose, music, film, and the like—and it is one of the only emotional experiences thought to be truly universal across cultures and societies. It is a primal, powerful force, love. Perhaps more than any other emotion, it drives us to turn our world upside down and to accomplish the incomprehensible for the sake of finding and keeping it. Whether it comes from a close friend, a child, or a life partner, love is an integral part of maintaining the strong social connections that are so vital to our survival.

Many of us rather enjoy the fact that love seems a mysterious force, one that defies rational explanation. We don't necessarily understand *why* we love this person or that one so much; we just do, and that's the beauty of it. Nothing about love needs to be logical—it is simply a part of the wondrous mystery that is the human experience. If you are such a person, here's fair warning that I will be spending the first part of this chapter demystifying love. It's a grand and wondrous experience, to be sure, but it turns out there's no real secret as to why we love. Knowing the answer to that question not only helps us understand why we love certain people (such as our children) more than other people (such as someone else's children); it also helps us see why affection hunger exists in the first place and can be so problematic when it isn't addressed.

If you prefer to retain the mystery of love, though, I completely respect that—and the story of affection deprivation will still make good sense to you if you decide to skip ahead to the section titled The Gift of Affection.

The (Real) Power of Love

Love may be many splendored, but for us humans it has a single, entirely nonromantic function: perpetuation of the species. If the emotion of love were to disappear tomorrow with nothing equally powerful to take its place, the human race would eventually go extinct.

To lay out the situation piece by piece:

1. Humans are born in a state of extreme dependence, unable to provide for themselves. They have no alternative but to rely on others to meet their needs.

2. Their needs are substantial. Not only are their economic needs considerable, but they require investments of virtually every other type of tangible and intangible resource that parents have to give.

3. Their period of dependence is significant. Humans do not have the cognitive development or motor ability to

provide completely for themselves until several years after their birth, which means they require an ongoing commitment of resources.

4. Something must sufficiently motivate adults—those who have the resources—to make the substantial and long-standing investment that ensures children's survival.

5. For humans, the motivator to invest in children is *love*. We willingly give our children all that we have, and then some, for the deceptively simple reason that *we love them so much*. We invest our lives—we sometimes even give our lives—for our children without ever seriously questioning why, because our love for them is so strong that we could not conceive of doing otherwise. And as a society, we reserve our harshest scorn for those who neglect, abuse, or otherwise break the covenant to love and protect young ones.

Love Is a Drive

We can think of love as sacred, spiritual, even trancendental, but in reality it is far more mundane than that. It is what psychologists call a *drive*, a state of tension that arises from a basic need and motivates us to do what is necessary to meet that need. For example, fatigue is a drive. Regular sleep is one of your body's basic needs, one you cannot survive without meeting, so to motivate you to get regular sleep, your body regularly produces the aversive state of fatigue. As you've been reminded every time you've tried to fight off fatigue, it's an unpleasant state that only gets worse over time until you finally succumb to it by doing what it is motivating you to do: get some sleep. Similarly, thirst is a drive, because we need to drink water to survive, and hunger is a drive, because we need to eat. Fatigue, thirst, and hunger all motivate behaviors necessary for our survival.

Love is also a drive, but the behaviors it motivates are not only for our *individual* survival. Love motivates us to meet the basic needs necessary to ensure the continuation of our species via the survival of our children. It is *the* motivator that ensures their well-being, just as fatigue is *the* motivator that ensures our sleep and hunger is *the* motivator that ensures our food intake. That is why we love—it's not terribly romantic, but when you consider that love keeps the human species from extinction, I think you'd agree it's pretty indispensible.

We Do More with Love Than Survive

Now, let's acknowledge that we do more in our lives with love than just keep the human race in existence. As an analogy, we have to eat to survive, but that doesn't mean we eat *only to* survive. Some of us are gloriously creative with food, making culinary masterpieces that are meant to be savored and enjoyed, not simply consumed for their nutritional content. Food features heavily in a wide range of cultural and religious traditions, and many holidays and other significant social events center around a shared meal. (I, for one, can't think about Thanksgiving without thinking about a turkey dinner.)

Preparing and sharing food, therefore, has far more meaning for humans than just the caloric intake necessary to sustain their bodies. The same observation can certainly be made about love. We need love to ensure the survival of children (and thus, the human race), but its meaning isn't limited to that. If it were, there wouldn't be so many poems and movies and Justin Bieber songs about it. Love has far more meaning for us than perpetuation of the species—even though perpetuation of the species is its primary function, just as the primary function of eating is simple caloric intake.

What kinds of love stories move you emotionally? What parts of your life—positive or negative—do they speak to?

That observation is critical because although we love our children dearly, they aren't the only people we love. They aren't the only people we need in our lives. Our social needs are more complex than that, and there isn't any one person, or any one type of relationship, capable of meeting them all. That's why we experience love in so many different forms.

Living Above the Line

Every one of our basic needs is subject to the same type of fundamental threshold:

minimum requirement met

---

minimum requirement unmet

No matter the specific need—whether food, water, shelter, and such—there's a minimum requirement necessary for our survival. Fail to meet that minimum and we will perish from starvation, thirst, exposure to the elements, or whatever specific threat the basic need addresses. However, once our minimum requirement is met—that is, once we're above the critical threshold—then the activity is able to support additional, secondary needs that aren't fundamental for surviving. As I described, so long as we're getting enough calories to sustain our bodies, we can use food to serve a wide range of cultural and religious traditions as well as personal needs (enjoying our favorite comfort foods when we're distressed) and professional ambitions (aquiring expertise in food preparation or evaluation as part of one's job). So long as we're adequately protected from the elements, we are above the threshold on our need for shelter and we no longer think of our homes as instruments of survival. We associate them with where we work or go to school, and where we raise our families. We think of our career trajectories and our financial health in terms of how much home we own, and where our houses are located. Our homes become symbols of status, pride, and identity.

Ask Yourself

How would you rate your own need for love? Rate your need on a scale of zero to ten, with zero being *very low* and ten being *very high*. How has your need for love changed over the past few years, if at all?

The great majority of us meet that minimum threshold of caring for children with room to spare: We have more than adequate love for our kids and they are not at risk of dying from neglect. This is certainly not to diminish the tragedy of child neglect and abuse, but simply to acknowledge the fortunate reality that it claims relatively few lives. Statistics released in 2010 from the

U.S. Department of Health and Human Services estimated that there were 1,560 child deaths that year that were attributable to neglect or abuse. Although that raw number is disturbing and should never be justified, it translates to a rate of 2.07 children per 100,000 children in the general population, meaning that the average child's likelihood of dying from neglect or abuse is 0.02 percent. That isn't 2 percent, it's two-hundredths of a percent. Although inexcusable, therefore, death by neglect and abuse is fortunately rare. For the most part, we meet our children's basic needs and live above the threshold.

Remember Cara, from the beginning of Chapter One? She realized what you probably understand already: She doesn't just want the love she feels from her son and husband—she needs it. How does she know she has it, though? How do any of us know that other people love us?

The answer, of course, is that people express their feelings of love and closeness to us through affectionate communication. They hug us and kiss us and hold our hand. They put their arms around us and squeeze us tight. They tell us how much they care about us. *That's* how we know we're loved. And those are the very behaviors that we miss and yearn for when we find ourselves in the grip of loneliness and affection hunger.

The Gift of Affection

You might never have wondered *why* humans show their affection to one other, but that's just the sort of quirk that academics like me fill our days thinking about. For me, specifically, this question has consumed much of my attention for the last two decades. After all, there's no denying how affectionate we are as a species. It's a big part of how we relate to each other—so much so that this tendency supports several different industries. Americans spend $7.5 billion on greeting cards every year, and an additional $32 billion on flowers, according to data from the Greeting Card Association and the Society of American Florists. Add in the candy, the jewelry, and all the other tokens of our fondness, and we have a cultural phenomenon crying out for explanation. As the National Retail Federation pointed out, Valentine's Day 2013 was the most expensive in history so far, with the average American shelling out $130.97 to spoil his or her sweetheart. Total spending was estimated at $18.6 billion for that holiday alone.

Good thing love itself is free.

What possesses us to do this—not just to buy the gifts and cards and trinkets of our love, but to communicate our love at all? What compels us to remind the important people in our lives *on a regular basis* how much we care about them?

The answer is deceptively simple: We learn it from our mothers.

We Can Thank Our Moms

Throughout the history of *Homo sapiens*, virtually all of us have had our childhood needs met primarily by the woman who gave us life, otherwise known as Mom. Many of the behaviors Mom used to meet our survival needs resemble actions we use today to communicate affection. Perhaps the easiest example to understand is the hug. Think of Cara, holding little Jacob close against her chest—and now think of a mother in prehistoric times doing the same to protect her infant from the bracing wind or to keep her newborn quiet and still during breastfeeding. Because the mother's body is many times the size of the baby's, she can envelop the baby to provide heat, stability, and protection, or to calm the baby when in distress. As I'll describe later in this book, this action releases stress-reducing chemicals in the bodies of both the mother and the child . . . and among others who repeat that action today in the form of a hug.

See, it's my belief that hugging—even the hugging we share with people at parties and church and graduation ceremonies—evolved over time from those protective, warmth-giving behaviors mothers have been using for millennia to keep their children safe and calm. What started as a mother's contribution to her children's survival, then, gradually became a gesture we use today to express our care for a much wider range of people in our lives.

Did You Know?

The lack of affection is related to violence. According to research, native cultures in which mothers frequently touch, hold, and carry their infants—such as the Maori of New Zealand and the Balinese from Indonesia—have the fewest incidents of violent crime. In such cultures, mothers maintain nearly constant contact with their infants by holding them close to their bodies and "wearing" them in baby carriers while working and socializing.

As another example—one that is perhaps not as readily apparent—consider the question of why we kiss. Once again it comes back to Mom, but not back to her kisses for affection. As with hugging, kissing also morphed out of a behavior mothers used to help ensure their infants' survival. Imagine a time in the distant past, long before there was Gerber, Bellamy's, or anything else remotely resembling baby food. Back then, moms did what birds do today—they chewed up food for their infants and passed it to them through their mouths. The technical term for this practice is *premastication*, and for infants born before the era of baby food, it was necessary for survival. Unlike a cougar cub, a human newborn doesn't have the teeth to chew up its food, let alone the motor coordination to use them, so Mom's pre-chewed meals provided the calories required to sustain their lives once they were weaned from her breast milk.

Indelicate as it may sound, the motor actions involved in moving chewed-up food from Mom's mouth to her child's are strikingly similar to those we use today when we kiss someone, especially sexually. In particular, French kissing—involving lip-on-lip and tongue-on-tongue contact—uses motor movements virtually identical to premastication.

Fortunately, We've Evolved

I'll be the first to admit that that sounds, well, less than romantic. Let me apologize in advance if, the next time you're kissing your sweetheart, the image of passing chewed-up food into his mouth wanders through your mind. Of course that isn't why we kiss today—or hug, or hold hands (as a mother would do to keep protective hold of her child), or do any of the other behaviors we use to show our affection for each other. We do them today for that very reason—to convey feelings of affection—but we use many of those particular movements, rather than others, because they've evolved over time from the caregiving we received that allowed each of us to survive our extended period of dependence.

Which physical forms of affection do you wish you received more often from others? Rank-order the following behaviors, starting with the one you most wish to receive more frequently:

1. Handholding
2. Kissing on lips
3. Putting arm around shoulder
4. Kissing on cheek
5. Hugging
6. Kissing on neck

Later in the chapter, you'll see how your results match those of a nationwide survey.

As a result of that process of "behavioral evolution," we find ourselves much like Cara. While she sits with her son in her arms and her husband beside her, she feels that she *needs* their love and affection—and not just the feeling of it, but also the *display* of it. She needs them to love her, but she also needs them to *show her that they love her*, if she is to be happy, emotionally healthy, fulfilled, and free of loneliness. It's an important realization on her part; fortunately, nature is way ahead of her. To ensure that she gets the amount of affection she needs, nature sees to it that she hungers after it. In moments such as this one, when her hunger is satisfied, she feels as calm and cared for as her newborn does in her arms. When she craves more affection than she gets, though, she feels unsettled, distressed, and lonely—and, as I'll explain in this book, her health can suffer in numerous ways. Satisfying our drive for affection—our affection hunger—is therefore as important for Cara, and all of us, as satisfying many of her other fundamental daily needs.

The Problem Is Common

If most of us receive enough love to live "above the line" and survive, then where does affection hunger come from? It obviously isn't the result of our not getting enough love to meet basic survival requirements. Someone gave us love adequate to sustain our existence, and we do the same for our children—so because we're above the threshold, love is now free to address many other needs not quite so grave as our survival. Our parents' love is vital to us, but it isn't nearly enough to meet our need to belong in this world. We also need friends and partners and a variety of social ties, both weak and strong. And, to avoid loneliness, we need to be able to give our love to more than just our children. We need peers and mentors, too. We need people who "get us." We need confidants and coconspirators, people who can share the burdens and the benefits of our lives. We need people who love us unconditionally yet tell us the truth about ourselves, and we need people who understand the value of simply being together in silence. Those people may be our parents or our children, our siblings or our cousins. They might be neighbors or coworkers, people we know from the synagogue or the gym or the PTA. They could be our lovers . . . current, former, or prospective. They may even be people we know only in virtual form, ones we've met and maintained relationships with online.

Sharing affectionate bonds with *anyone* who matters to us is a benefit, whether it contributes directly to the survival of our species or not. Unfortunately, it's a benefit many of us are lacking: Even though we're above the minimum threshold for survival, many of us still feel a persistent need for more loving affection than we get. That's the hunger in affection hunger.

Just how widespread a problem is this affection hunger, anyway? A couple of years ago, I got an interesting opportunity to find out. I received a call from the marketing department at the skin-care products company Nivea. Maybe you know Nivea: They make hand cream and lip balm and all manner of goods meant to improve the look and feel of your skin. I've used their aftershave lotion for years. "Touch and Be Touched" is their current slogan—which, cleverly enough, encourages an ongoing need for their product line.

As the caller explained that day, Nivea wanted to launch a new public relations campaign promoting "A Million Moments of Touch." The idea was that they would tout the benefits of close, affectionate touch and would actually get people to record their moments of touch on a Facebook page in exchange for chances to win prizes. To help make the case that people should touch more often, Nivea asked me to conduct a survey of American adults to find out how affection deprived we really are. Although my research is normally of the academic variety, I accepted the chance to do some opinion polling and find out how Americans really felt about affection and affectionate touch.

I created a survey, posted it online, and had nearly 1,500 responses within a few days. The participants, all adults, came from every geographic region of the United States and represented every ethnic group, economic class, and relationship status. It's not technically a random sample of Americans—the kind we see in major political polls, for example—but it contained enough diversity to give me confidence in the results.

Here's an overview of some of my findings:

- Three out of four adults agree that "Americans are in a state of affection hunger." Women and men were equally likely to endorse this statement.
- We touch our cell phones more often than we touch each other. 57.2 percent of Americans say they touch their cell phones "always or quite a bit," whereas 28.6 percent say they touch a family member and 16.7 percent say they touch their closest friend always or quite a bit.
- When asked which forms of physical affection they wished to receive more often than they do, people said:

  1. Handholding (60.2%)
  2. Hugging (59.6%)
  3. Arm around shoulder (46.0%)
  4. Kissing on cheek (34.5%)
  5. Kissing on lips (25.4%)
  6. Kissing on neck (20.3%)

- Among regions of the United States, those most likely to agree that Americans are affection deprived were Hawaii (100 percent), the South (85 percent), and the Central Plains (82 percent). In no region of the country was agreement with that claim less than 50 percent.

As you can see, the results were diverse but they weren't ambiguous. The concept of affection hunger clearly struck a chord with Americans, who agreed overwhelmingly that they felt it.

Did You Know?

People in cold climates receive the least touch. According to research, people who live closest to the equator (where climates are warmer) touch each other more than those who live farther from the equator.

You might identify with one or more of the findings in my survey. Perhaps you, too, agree with the idea that affection hunger is a problem. Maybe you find yourself in contact with your cell phone or your laptop or your TV remote more often than with your loved ones. That's common, and if you crave more intimacy than you get, then you have probably tried more than one way of increasing the amount of affection in your life. That's easier said than done, as you likely know. One reason why is that people aren't always receptive to affectionate behavior. When it comes at the wrong time, from the wrong person, or in the wrong form, it doesn't wash over you like a comforting wave of love. Instead, it can feel more like a wave that's out to drown you.

A Time and a Place

"To every thing there is a season," wrote King Solomon, and the communication of affection is no exception. As we consider how important it is to our health and well-being, let's also remember that—as with many other things that matter to us—there's a time and a place for it.

Given at the right time, in the right way, within the right relationship, affectionate behavior can transform our day—or our life—in supremely positive ways. Of course that isn't an argument to begin kissing strangers on the street. We know from experience, if not intuition, what bad advice that would be, but let's take a moment to think about why. If affection is good some of the time, why isn't it good all of the time?

Affection Can Be Unwelcome

When I was in college I used to work during the summers as a temp, spending a week at this company and a week at that one, usually doing some type of office work. I could type fast and had actually learned to write shorthand in school, so I got some pretty plum assignments working for high-level executives. On one weeklong assignment I was working for a manager we'll call Rick. He was a friendly sort, very gregarious, and, I noticed, very touchy. He couldn't talk to someone without touching that person in some way—he'd put his hand on their shoulder, squeeze their arm, shake their hand using both of his, whatever.

Now, let me say that I'm very much the same way. I like to touch people when I visit with them, and I find folks who are similar to be generally warm and compassionate individuals. Thus, I didn't mind this part of Rick's personality at all. I didn't mind it, that is, until he hugged me one afternoon in his office and wouldn't let go. There are really only two contexts in which something like that would occur—and he wasn't in emotional distress and needing a sympathetic ear. Trust me, it wasn't my ear he was after.

Maria's Story

MARIA WANTS MORE AFFECTION IN HER LIFE IN GENERAL, BUT IN SOME SITUATIONS, AFFECTION MAKES HER UNCOMFORTABLE. AT WORK, FOR INSTANCE, SHE HAS A TOUCHY-FEELY BOSS WHO LIKES TO HUG HIS EMPLOYEES. MARIA DOESN'T MIND THAT, SO LONG AS HER BOSS INTERACTS THAT WAY WITH EVERYONE. ON OCCASION, THOUGH, HE HUGS HER WHEN THEY'RE ALONE IN THE OFFICE, AND THAT MAKES HER VERY UNCOMFORTABLE. SHE CERTAINLY DOESN'T WANT TO GET HER BOSS IN TROUBLE, AS SHE GENERALLY APPRECIATES HIS AFFECTIONATE NATURE. SHE JUST WISHES HE'D SAVE HIS HUGS FOR THOSE TIMES WHEN OTHERS ARE AROUND.

Maybe you've been in a similar situation. It could have been with a stranger, or someone you barely knew (as with Rick and me). It might have been with a close acquaintance, a boss (as in Maria's case), or someone you knew quite well. It may even have been a very close friend who chose to express romantic feelings for you. Whatever the specifics, you can probably remember feeling much the same way I did in Rick's office. The technical term for that feeling is *creeped out.*

Affection Can Be Harmful

In cases such as those, the affectionate behavior we receive is hardly a boon to our health and well-being. It might, actually, be just the opposite. When we receive gestures of unwelcome affection, we experience a stress response. In essence, our bodies perceive they are being endangered, and they go into defensive protection mode. Think about that: A hug, which would certainly bring me joy and make me feel loved if received from, say, my brother, was in this instance causing my body to feel it was being threatened.

Threatened by a hug?

Sounds strange to say, but I bet you know exactly what I mean. Affectionate behavior that comes to us when we don't want it, or in a manner that we don't like, or from a person we don't welcome it from, is stress inducing. It makes us feel unsafe, even violated. The reason is that although we humans need affection for survival, we didn't evolve to need it just anytime or from just anyone. "To every thing there is a season," and we have developed to need affection within a specific window.

Just ask anyone who's experienced sexual harassment in the workplace, for example, or been the victim of stalking or the target of unrequited love. People in those situations receive some form of attention—often *overtly* affectionate in nature—that they do not welcome. Many victims of harassment and stalking are forced to take legal action against perpetrators and require medical and psychotherapeutic treatment to manage the emotional effects. Being the target of unrequited love may not be as dramatic, but research by psychologist Roy Baumeister shows it too is enormously stressful, even more stressful than for the one whose love is rejected. This type of stress and alienation can, in fact, *cause* loneliness, if it makes the person wary of future social interactions.

Ask Yourself

When have you felt stressed by an affectionate expression? How did it make you feel, physically and emotionally?

Clearly, then, getting affection we don't want can be uncomfortable and distressing. Not getting the affection we *do* want and need can be disastrous, though, and that's unfortunately the situation so many Americans find themselves in today. There's a striking irony here, in that we have more ways to express affection to each other than at any other time in our history, yet as our options increase in number, they seem to decrease in value.

Is Technology the Problem?

It happens that I'm writing this section of this chapter on my birthday. As I'm sitting in front of my monitor typing, my computer keeps chiming every time someone posts a birthday message on my Facebook wall. If you're a Facebook user, you know what I'm talking about—by the end of the day I'll probably have a few dozen such postings, the vast majority of which will say "Happy Birthday!" and nothing more.

Believe me when I say I appreciate that each of those people took a moment out of their day to think of me and connect with me in a friendly manner. I myself have done the same on numerous occasions—and it's because I've done the same that I understand the genuine meaning of the gesture. This is a time for honesty, so I'll throw myself under the bus: In most cases, I don't even know it's the person's birthday until Facebook reminds me, and typing "Happy Birthday!" on their wall is an empty-calorie gesture, easy to do but devoid of much real meaning. That isn't always the case, of course. When it's a close friend or relative, the message is meaningful and Facebook may simply be the most efficient medium for communicating it.

On one hand, then, I might go through the dozens of posts on my wall and be amazed at how much affection I have received, but I know better than that, and so do you. I know which messages are meaningful and how many are pro forma. And at the end of the day, that doesn't leave me wishing for another hundred messages, but rather for contact, conversation, touch, and time together with the three or four people whose affection means the most to me.

Why not blame Facebook itself for the problem, then? If we didn't make it so easy to shoot off meaningless messages of empty affect, we could return to the days of genuine human connection. Maybe it's Twitter's fault. For that matter, let's point the finger at the Internet at large—before that came along, people really *talked* to each other, didn't they?

Communication technology certainly isn't irrelevant, but there's an enormous logical problem in blaming it for our troubles: It didn't arise on its own. It doesn't do anything on its own. *We created it.* We can't say that technology separates us, because that treats technology as a living, breathing thing, which it isn't. All we can say is that *we separate ourselves through technology.* And that's true, but acknowledging it isn't enough to make things better. The Blame Game never gets us far—what we need are solutions, ones based on the best available research. Just as medical scientists study, say, the benefits of exercise or the dangers of malnutrition, social scientists (including myself) have been studying the benefits and risks of affection as a way to understand its importance in human social interaction.

Technology isn't the problem . . . we are. We need love and affection in our lives, yet we often feel deprived of those very experiences, leading to a state of loneliness and affection hunger.

Did You Know?

It's possible to have *too many* Facebook friends. According to research, Facebook users start appearing less desirable and popular when they have more than 300 friends. One possible reason why is that most of us can't maintain high-quality relationships with that many people, so having several hundred Facebook friends can make someone look shallow or hungry for attention.

Feeling Affection Deprived

The concept of *deprivation* means receiving less of something than you desire. You're deprived of food when you don't get enough to satisfy your hunger. You feel sleep deprived when you can't catch enough shuteye to feel rested. When it comes to identifying deprivation, therefore, we have to consider and compare two things: the amount of something you desire, and the amount you receive.

Although it's easy to focus only on how much affection we get or don't get, that's only half the story. For example, suppose that Naomi—a twenty-seven-year-old divorced Caucasian woman—and Jonathan—a thirty-eight-year-old married African American man—both score 4.5 on a ten-point scale when asked to rate how much affection they receive. Can we conclude that they feel equally affection deprived?

We cannot, until we know how much they want. Even though Naomi and Jonathan receive equal amounts of affection, it's possible that Naomi feels a much higher level of deprivation. That would be the case if she *wants* more affection than Jonathan does.

In other words, it isn't just *how much we want* or *how much we get* that determines how deprived we feel—it's the difference between those amounts. To determine their levels of deprivation, we would also have to ask Naomi and Jonathan how much affection they wish they received. As the following figure shows, even though Naomi and Jonathan receive the same amount of affection, Naomi feels more deprived because she has a larger discrepancy between the amount she wants and the amount she gets.

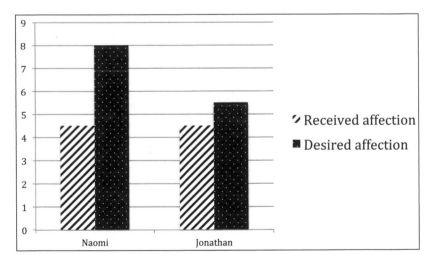

Different levels of affection deprivation

Naomi and Jonathan both report their "received affection" score as 4.5. Naomi, however, wishes that her received affection level were 8.0, whereas Jonathan wishes that his level were only

5.5. Even though they receive the same amount of affection from others, therefore, Naomi feels more deprived.

These observations are important because they show how variable affection hunger can be from person to person. Some of us get more food, more sleep, and more affection than others do—but not everyone needs the same amounts, either. It's when we receive substantially less than we desire that we truly feel deprived. And as the upcoming chapters explain, we benefit when our affection needs are met, and we suffer when they aren't.

Stop and Reflect

We've talked in this chapter about where our need for affection comes from, why unwanted expressions of affection can be stressful, and how technology can cheapen our experience in relationships. Before moving on to Chapter Three, take a few minutes to reflect on these questions, writing out your responses so you can reference them later.

- How important is love to you? What things do you do to gain, grow, or avoid losing love?
- When have you received unwanted affection from someone you knew? How would you describe the emotional and physical feelings you experienced?
- In what ways do you separate yourself through technology from people you care about?

CHAPTER THREE

How Affection Helps

Affectionate relationships are one of the cornerstones of a healthy human life. If you feel lonely and in need of more substantial human contact, you are probably also missing out on the many benefits that affection can provide, both physically and mentally. Showing affection in relationships is about more than just sharing Valentine's Day cards and hugs—it offers tangible, measurable improvements to your body and mind.

Anyone who's raised a child in the last few decades might be surprised to learn that, prior to the mid-twentieth century, experts warned parents against showing affection to their children. Psychologists argued that it would make children needy and demanding, and doctors cautioned that it would promote the spread of infectious diseases. That view went largely unchallenged until Harry Harlow became interested in monkeys.

Harlow was a Stanford-trained psychologist who established one of the first primate laboratories in the world at the University of Wisconsin. His experiments—although they severely strained the limits of what we would consider ethical animal treatment today—were truly pioneering in what they taught us about the necessity of affection. In his work, Harlow separated baby rhesus monkeys from their mothers and situated them in his lab to be "raised" by two types of machines designed to resemble surrogate monkey moms. One mother was covered with heavy mesh wire, the kind someone might use to fashion a cage for chickens. The other, although also crafted from wire, was covered with thick, soft terrycloth, the type a fluffy bath towel is made of.

In his now-classic experiments, Harlow divided his rhesus infants into two groups. For the first group, the wire mother dispensed food and the terrycloth mother did not, whereas for the second group, the opposite was true. Regardless of the circumstance, Harlow saw the same pattern of behavior: The babies clung to the terrycloth mother whether it provided food or not, and would visit the wire mother only when they needed to eat. In his later studies, he would expose the monkeys to stressful stimuli, such as a noise-making teddy bear, and he found that, virtually without exception, the babies would cling to their terrycloth mothers for comfort. When he denied them that opportunity by removing the cloth-covered apparatus from their environments, the rhesus infants quickly demonstrated signs of physical and psychological distress, such as disengaging, curling up in a ball, and sucking their thumbs.

Did You Know?

Harlow's research helped effect key changes in how orphanages and adoption agencies cared for children.

Although we now consider it unduly cruel to the animals involved, Harlow's research was nonetheless groundbreaking in demonstrating both the need for attachment and the consequences of denying that need. Humans aren't rhesus monkeys, of course—but according to Dr. Phyllis Leppert of the U.S. National Institutes of Health, we have approximately 95 percent of our DNA in common with them. That genetic similarity matters, because it elevates the odds that we share with monkeys various central nervous system structures that make attachment behaviors (such as sharing comfort and affection) similarly rewarding to us.

If that's true—if our bodies are, in a sense, hardwired to benefit from comforting, affectionate interaction—then it is logical to expect a close relationship between affection and our health and well-being. Before I describe the specifics of that relationship, let me explain what it can teach us about affection hunger. Up to this point in the book, I have focused the discussion on *why* affection is so important to us as humans: because none of us would have survived our infancy without it. It doesn't cease to be valuable to us once we grow up, though. We all continue to need affection throughout our lives, because we experience many important benefits when we have it and because we suffer when we lack it. My purpose in this chapter is to describe *how* that's true.

To explore the benefits of having affection and the detriments of lacking it, it helps to think of affectionate behavior as both a state and a trait.

Affection as a State and a Trait

Each of us can be described as having a mix of states and traits.

- A **state** is a characteristic that defines us on occasion. Normally we think of states as attributes we have from time to time, such as being angry, being hungry, or being amused. States can also be behavioral, such as when we are feeling particularly talkative, especially jittery, or very physically active. No matter the specifics, a state is temporal, usually lasting only for a short while.

- In comparison, a **trait** is a more enduring feature. Our traits describe who we are and what we do under most circumstances. Some of our traits are physical or psychological, such as our eye color or intelligence, and others are behavioral, such as how friendly or competitive we are. Whenever you hear someone referred to as "an aggressive person" or "a good listener," you're hearing about that person's traits.

Behavioral states and traits overlap each other substantially, but not entirely. I once had a neighbor named Clara who was one of the most talkative people I've ever met. She could chat up just about anyone, from her bank teller to our letter carrier to the young man who rotated her tires—and once you got into a conversation with Clara, it was hard to escape. I confess there were times when I would see her through my kitchen window and intentionally wait until she had left before walking out to my car, in order to avoid getting trapped in another seemingly endless chat.

As a "talkative person," therefore, Clara talked a lot, and in many social situations, not just a few. Having a talkative trait therefore led her to experience many talkative states. That didn't necessarily mean she was chatty—or equally chatty—with everyone, though. Despite her trait, Clara probably found herself in a quiet, nontalkative state from time to time . . . just not as often as the rest of us.

We can make the same distinction about affection. Each of us is affectionate in some relationships, and in some situations, more than in others. Maybe you hug your parents a bit more tightly than your in-laws, for example. Sometimes you feel like cuddling with your romantic partner, and sometimes you don't. There's variation in how affectionately each of us behaves as we go through life—yet it's also true that certain people are just more affectionate than others overall. Some of us are very touchy-feely, always expressing our love and appreciation for others, and feeling comfortable around people who do the same. Others of us live on the opposite end of that continuum, either uncomfortable showing our affection for people or just not experiencing the need for it. That doesn't mean that less-affectionate people don't *feel* love and appreciation; it simply means they aren't prone to expressing it.

Kenny's Story

WITHIN TWO MONTHS OF MOVING IN WITH HIS PARTNER AARON, KENNY REALIZED HOW MUCH THEY DIFFERED IN THEIR TENDENCIES TOWARD AFFECTION. HE HADN'T NOTICED IT AS MUCH WHEN THEY STARTED DATING, BUT NOW THAT THEY LIVE TOGETHER, KENNY HAS DISCOVERED THAT HE'S MUCH MORE AFFECTIONATE ON A DAY-TO-DAY BASIS THAN AARON IS. AT FIRST, KENNY FOUND THIS DISTRESSING, BECAUSE HE ASSUMED THAT IF AARON DIDN'T *SHOW* AS MUCH AFFECTION AS HE DID, THEN HE DIDN'T *FEEL* AS MUCH. THAT FEAR CAUSED KENNY TO WORRY THAT THEY WEREN'T A GOOD FIT FOR EACH OTHER, ESPECIALLY IN THE LONG TERM. HE NOW REALIZES, THOUGH,

THAT HE IS MORE EXPRESSIVE THAN AARON ABOUT MOST EMOTIONS, NOT JUST AFFECTIONATE ONES, AND HE UNDERSTANDS THAT IT IS MERELY A DIFFERENCE IN HOW THEY ACT, NOT HOW THEY FEEL. AARON IS SIMPLY MORE RESERVED WHEN IT COMES TO EXPRESSING HIMSELF. BY TALKING WITH AARON, KENNY CAME TO UNDERSTAND THAT AARON REALLY DOES LOVE HIM; HE JUST ISN'T AS DEMONSTRATIVE AS KENNY IS.

Like Kenny and Aaron, each of us has a trait level of affectionate behavior that represents how affectionate we typically are. Regardless of what our individual level is, each of us also finds ourselves in affectionate states from time to time, in which we express our feelings of fondness and love for others. If it's true that we're hardwired to benefit from giving and receiving affection—as Harlow's studies first suggested—then it is likely that those benefits follow both from *being an affectionate person* (as a trait) and from *sharing affectionate behavior* (as a state). As it turns out, each of these predictions is true.

Being an Affectionate Person Is Healthy

From time to time, we all have "one of those days," and the other day was certainly one of mine. It was the first day of summer school and I was teaching an undergraduate course about nonverbal communication—the many ways we express and share meaning without the use of words. I normally teach in the afternoons, but this was a morning class, which required me to drive to campus during rush hour. On this particular morning, there were two separate accidents on the eight-mile stretch of freeway between my house and my office, so by the time I got to school, I was already frazzled. While sitting in my office before class, I received a phone call from my doctor with some very bad health news. Feeling preoccupied and overwhelmed, I didn't notice when the time to begin teaching came and went. A timid knock on my door several minutes later from a student made me realize I was nearly fifteen minutes late for class . . . something I always try to avoid, especially on the first day of school. Flustered, I grabbed my lecture notes and water bottle and ran downstairs to my classroom. As I rushed in, I put my notes and bottle on the front table and promptly spilled my water over everything, even as I was apologizing profusely for my lateness. A few minutes later, while pulling on the cord to bring down the screen for my PowerPoint projector, a student pointed out that the screen was operated electrically. Pretending I knew that, I walked over to the wall to flip the switch that would lower the screen, but I flipped the wrong switch and turned out all the lights in the room. This comedy of errors all transpired during my first three minutes in front of my new class.

Given the combination of a rough commute, some very bad health news, and an embarrassing first day of teaching, I was feeling pretty low by the time I returned to my office. Fortunately one of my colleagues and dear friends spotted me in the hallway and, having quickly assessed my condition, asked "Do you need a hug?" "Yes, very much," I replied. It ended up being exactly what I needed at exactly the right time.

When my colleague put her arms around me in the hallway, it didn't change anything about what had gone wrong in my day. However, it changed *everything* about the way I felt. I relaxed. The tense, stressful feelings that had enveloped me all morning began to melt away. My frustrating drive to work, my worrisome phone call with the doctor, and my calamitous class session were still fresh in my mind, but suddenly they all seemed less disastrous. After the hug from my friend, I felt I could cope with the morning's problems and face whatever was yet to come that day. That hug lowered my experience of stress, both emotionally and physically.

Did You Know?

Receiving affectionate touch from a spouse reduces our blood pressure and stress hormones.

In retrospect, that's a pretty substantial effect for such a small, short-lived behavior. I doubt our hug lasted more than two seconds before it was over—yet its positive effects on me were definitely noticeable and longer lasting. Maybe you can recall a situation in your own life when even a small gesture of affection—a hug, a phone call, an arm around the shoulder—changed your mental and physical state for the better. Why do affectionate behaviors bring these benefits?

Harlow (who studied the monkey babies) was among the first researchers to gather scientific evidence on the benefits of affectionate contact. Since his time, we have learned much more about *how* affection is good for us, and one of the conclusions we can draw from this work is that people who give and receive a great deal of affection are in better mental and physical health than people who give and receive less affection. In other words, there are benefits to being a highly affectionate person. In fact, people who are high in trait affection are both happier and healthier than the rest of us.

How Affectionate Are You?

Take a moment to look at the following statements. Consider how much you agree or disagree with each item by assigning it a number between 1 and 7. Assign a higher number if you agree more, and a lower number if you agree less.

- I CONSIDER MYSELF TO BE A VERY AFFECTIONATE PERSON. _____
- I AM ALWAYS TELLING MY LOVED ONES HOW MUCH I CARE ABOUT THEM. _____
- WHEN I FEEL AFFECTION FOR SOMEONE, I USUALLY EXPRESS IT. _____
- I RARELY HAVE A HARD TIME TELLING PEOPLE THAT I LOVE THEM OR CARE ABOUT THEM. _____
- I'M PRETTY GOOD AT EXPRESSING AFFECTION. _____
- I'M A VERY AFFECTIONATE PERSON. _____
- I LOVE GIVING PEOPLE HUGS OR PUTTING MY ARMS AROUND THEM. _____
- I TEND TO EXPRESS AFFECTION TO OTHER PEOPLE QUITE OFTEN. _____
- EXPRESSING AFFECTION TO OTHER PEOPLE RARELY MAKES ME UNCOMFORTABLE. _____
- ANYONE WHO KNOWS ME WELL WOULD SAY THAT I'M PRETTY AFFECTIONATE. _____

Once you've assigned a number between 1 and 7 to each item, add your numbers together. Your total score should be between 10 and 70.

(These items originally appeared in Floyd, K. (2002). Human affection exchange: V. Attributes of the highly affectionate. *Communication Quarterly*, 50: 135–154. Reproduced with permission.)

Affectionate People Have Better Mental Health

Before proceeding, take the "How Affectionate Are You?" quiz. These items come from a questionnaire measure called the Trait Affection Scale, which I developed as a way to assess people's trait affection levels in research. As you might imagine, not very many people score at the extremes of 10 or 70. In other words, most of us aren't extremely affectionate or completely non-affectionate, but we live somewhere in between, not shying away from affection but not being overly expressive, either. The higher your score, though, the more affectionate you are as a person. And there are several advantages to having a high trait affection level.

A decade ago, I conducted what was probably the first study to examine the benefits that went along with being a highly affectionate person. My method was quite simple. I prepared two identical versions of a questionnaire that included a battery of mental health assessments, personality measures, and scales about the quality of people's relationships. The questionnaire also included a version of the trait affection scale that you just completed for yourself. I then handed out the pairs of questionnaires to students at my university and offered them extra course credit for giving the questionnaires to the "most affectionate person you know" and the "least affectionate person you know." Each questionnaire was attached to a postage-paid return envelope (this was before it was easy to do surveys online), so students earned their extra credit if they were able to persuade two people they knew to fill out and return the questionnaires. Most of the students told me they had no problem thinking of people—both highly affectionate and non-affectionate—to approach for this task.

What this method gave me, then, was data from two groups of people I already knew would differ in their trait affection levels. And indeed they did—remember your total score from the ten-item scale? In this study, the people in my high-affection group had an average total score of 64 out of 70, which means my students did a great job of finding me highly affectionate people. In contrast, the people in my low-affection group had an average total score of only 33. The two groups certainly differed in how affectionate they were, and what I wanted to find out was: How else did they differ from each other?

The answer I found was that highly affectionate people were not only different, but *advantaged*, relative to their low-affection counterparts on virtually every outcome I measured. I'll focus here on outcomes relevant to their mental health and well-being. Compared to low-affection communicators, highly affectionate people:

- Experienced less stress, less depression, and more happiness
- Enjoyed higher self-esteem
- Felt less lonely
- Were more likely to be socially active
- Felt more secure about their personal relationships, more comfortable with emotional closeness, and less fearful of intimacy

To put it plainly, highly affectionate people are in better mental health than less-affectionate people, according to the results of that study. A few years later, in an attempt to gain more certainty about these comparisons, several colleagues and I did three further studies. We repeated most of the findings I had already identified, and we also found that highly affectionate people were less neurotic, less psychotic, more extraverted, and more likely to have loving, satisfying relationships.

The mental and relational benefits of being highly affectionate aren't limited to Americans, either. When you look around the world, it is certainly true that some cultures are more affectionate than others. The variation is especially noticeable when you look at touch. Researchers call some cultures *high-contact cultures* because it is common for people in those groups to touch each other often, and in very familiar, even intimate ways. Mediterranean countries, such as Italy and Greece, are great examples. In that region of the world, it is both common and expected for people to touch each other, in both affectionate ways and more instrumental ways (such as helping someone across the street). People in high-contact cultures maintain a smaller "bubble" of personal, private space, preferring to give and receive high levels of touch with each other. In comparison, *low-contact cultures* are those in which very little interpersonal touch is observed or expected.

One study by communication researchers Ed McDaniel and Peter Andersen that included participants from twenty-five countries found that China, Japan, and Korea were the lowest-contact cultures in the world. Most researchers would classify the United States as a *medium-contact culture*, although some parts of the country (such as the South) are certainly higher-contact areas than others (such as the Midwest).

Bruce's Story

AS A DISTRIBUTION MANAGER FOR A LARGE INTERNATIONAL MANUFACTURING FIRM, BRUCE TRAVELS FREQUENTLY FOR WORK. IN SOME COUNTRIES, HE HAS DISCOVERED THAT IT IS CUSTOMARY FOR MEN TO GREET HIM BY KISSING HIM ON THE CHEEK. HE USUALLY DOESN'T HAVE A PROBLEM GETTING USED TO OTHER CULTURES AND THEIR TRADITIONS, BUT HE FOUND THAT THIS PARTICULAR PRACTICE MADE HIM VERY UNCOMFORTABLE. HE MENTIONED HIS DISCOMFORT TO A COLLEAGUE WHO ALSO TRAVELS FREQUENTLY, AND SHE HELPED HIM UNDERSTAND THAT IN SUCH CULTURES, KISSING ON THE CHEEK IS NOT AN EXPRESSION OF AFFECTION, PER SE. RATHER, IT'S A ROUTINE, OBLIGATORY SOCIAL GREETING, JUST LIKE A HANDSHAKE IS BETWEEN AMERICANS. BRUCE DIDN'T GET OVER HIS DISCOMFORT IMMEDIATELY, BUT HE EVENTUALLY GOT USED TO THE PRACTICE BY THINKING OF IT AS SIMILAR TO A HANDSHAKE, NOT AN AFFECTIONATE EXPRESSION.

It stands to reason that being an affectionate person is beneficial in a culture that accepts and practices high levels of affection— but what about in a low-contact culture? Recently, psychologist Michael Shengtau Wu and I wanted to see how American and Chinese adults differed from each other in their levels of trait affection and in the benefits associated with it. With the help of several bilingual speakers, we translated the Trait Affection Scale into Mandarin and distributed it to several hundred adults in both China and the United States, along with measures of mental wellness. As we expected, Chinese adults scored much lower on trait affection than did Americans, a reflection of the low-contact nature of the Chinese culture. Importantly, however, we found that being affectionate is just as strongly associated with mental health benefits for Chinese adults as for Americans. Specifically, highly affectionate participants—whether Chinese or American—had higher self-esteem, more satisfaction with life, more positive affect, and greater resilience in the face of stress. They were also more empathic, more likely to have close relationships, and less likely to be relationship avoidant.

Based on our findings, we can say that being a highly affectionate person is associated with better mental and relational well-being, regardless of whether affectionate contact is common in your culture or not. That's good to know, but in retrospect it may not be very surprising. I've spent a fair amount of this book discussing what an inherently social species we humans are, so it's not really a revelation that those who interact affectionately with others are less stressed and depressed than those who don't. It's in our nature. Even if these mental well-being studies weren't groundbreaking, they did give me reason to push my curiosity further, by asking whether highly affectionate people are also healthier physically.

Affectionate People Have Better Physical Health

I first suspected that being affectionate would relate to physical health, you'll recall, because sharing affection *feels good*—and it doesn't just feel good emotionally or psychologically. It feels good physically. It warms us and eases us and floods our bodies with peaceful sensations. And in particular, it helps us when we're stressed, as that hug from my colleague did for me when it was "one of those days." I've thought about this for a long time, the fact that this communication behavior—affection—affects our bodies and makes us feel good. I don't believe it's a coincidence or an accident of nature, any more than it's a fluke that eating and sleeping both feel good. And if I'm right about that, then the possibility exists that affection *feels good to us* because it *is good for us*.

My exploration of that idea began with a study in which I predicted that the bodies of highly affectionate people manage stress more effectively than the bodies of less-affectionate people. Because the physical benefits of affection seem especially pronounced during times of stress (such as when a hug on a stressful morning calms me down), I decided that looking at the body's stress response would be a good place to start examining the role of affection in physical health. On top of that, stress is something we all deal with, and it's associated with a wide range of other problems—from obesity, high blood pressure, asthma, and heart disease, to headaches, sleep disorders, depression, high cholesterol, and diabetes. To me, that alone made stress worthwhile to study, because helping people manage stress more effectively can lead to improvements in the types of conditions that get exacerbated by stress.

Ask Yourself

Which health problems—such as poor sleep, headaches, or digestion problems—are made worse when you feel stressed?

Measuring Stress

How does one measure the body's ability to manage stress? One of the most common ways is to look at the production of a hormone called *cortisol*. Cortisol is produced by the adrenal glands, which sit atop each of the kidneys, and it follows a twenty-four-hour cycle called a diurnal rhythm (the word *diurnal* means "about a day"). For most of us, our cortisol levels are at their highest within thirty minutes of awakening. That's their peak. They drop sharply throughout the morning and early afternoon, and they continue to drop during the late afternoon and evening, although not as quickly. Usually they reach their lowest point around midnight, then begin the climb back upward for the next morning's peak. That's a normal, healthy diurnal rhythm.

The more variation we have in our diurnal rhythm, the better, because that signals that we have a healthy *hypothalamic-pituitary-adrenal (HPA) axis*, one of the major systems in our bodies that respond to stressful events. When the HPA axis is dysregulated—that is, less able to respond effectively to stressful occurrences—our diurnal rhythm for cortisol loses variation. It "flattens out," so to speak. Therefore, a flat cortisol rhythm indicates a body that is poorly equipped to manage stressful situations, whereas more variation in the cortisol rhythm indicates a body that is ready to respond to stressful events when they occur.

In my first study of cortisol, I had a group of healthy adult volunteers fill out the Trait Affection Scale and then collect samples of their saliva at four points in time during a normal workday: when they first woke up, at noon, in the late afternoon, and when they went to bed. I used the saliva samples to measure their cortisol levels at these four time points, which allowed me to graph each individual's cortisol rhythm over the course of the day. When I compared each person's rhythm to his or her trait affection level, I found what I expected: The more affectionate someone was, the greater the variation in his or her cortisol levels over the day.

Examining the Stress Response

We can therefore say that trait affection is linked to the body's readiness to manage stress—but what happens when we actually encounter stressful events? Does being a highly affectionate person help you deal with stressful situations in the moment?

Answering that question is a bit more involved than having people fill out some forms and provide spit samples. To see how affectionate and non-affectionate people deal with stressful events, I need to observe them during episodes of stress. It isn't enough simply to ask people what goes on in their bodies when they're stressed out, because much of what the body experiences during those times is outside of our conscious awareness. Think about it: When you encounter a stressful episode, you may notice your heart beating faster, your face feeling hot, and your muscles feeling tense, but you probably couldn't tell *how much* your heart rate, skin temperature, or muscle tension have increased. You also don't know how your cortisol levels have changed or how your immune system is responding. These physical activities are simply beyond our awareness—so to study them involves measuring them under conditions of stress.

And for the sake of research, that requires us to stress people out on purpose.

If you were a participant in one of these studies, I would ask you to fill out the Trait Affection Scale and then make an appointment to visit our lab. Once there, you would be put through forty-five minutes of activities that are designed to stress you out. There would be a mental math challenge, in which you are given math problems to solve in your head while a research assistant stands over your shoulder pointing out your wrong answers. You'd do a

Stroop color word test, in which you see names of colors flash on a computer screen written in colors different from the one being named—so, the word *yellow* written in purple letters, for instance. In the Stroop test, you have to call out the color of the letters, not the color being named in the word. The words flash quickly and in an unexpected pattern, and it's easy to get flustered.

You would plunge your entire forearm into a bucket of ice water and hold it there for a couple of minutes. That may not sound emotionally stressful, but it produces an immediate stress reaction physically. You'd also watch videos of spouses fighting and screaming at each other. After doing each activity a couple of times, your overall stress level would be pretty high, and we would monitor how your body reacts during this entire encounter.

Thankfully, people actually volunteer for these kinds of studies—and because they do, we've learned a bit about how affectionate and non-affectionate people react differently. The general pattern is this: The more affection people give and receive, the less likely they are to overreact to stressful situations.

Understanding why that's an advantage requires us to appreciate the role of stress in our lives. Most of us think of stress in the same way we think of death and taxes: as one of life's unpleasant certainties. Few people enjoy the experience of stress—but like the experience of a mammogram or prostate exam, it is a necessary component of our wellness. That's because stress is the body's response to any type of perceived threat, and if we don't respond adequately to threats, we quickly become vulnerable to them.

To understand your body's stress response, let's imagine that while taking your evening walk, you turn a corner and find yourself face to face with a growling German shepherd, ears back and teeth bared. Given its ability to issue a painful bite—and its apparent readiness to do so—the dog certainly represents a threat. The presence of the dog is a *stressor*, and your body reacts to it by experiencing *stress*. Your heart starts pounding, your breathing gets heavier, and your muscles become tense. Outside your conscious awareness, the pupils of your eyes dilate, your blood supply gets redirected, your body starts pumping out stress hormones, and your immune system kicks into high gear. All of these changes have the same function: to help you survive the threat you're facing. You breathe faster to get more oxygen into your bloodstream, which your rapidly beating heart distributes quickly to fuel your muscles. Muscles become tense to protect you from a physical impact and to prepare you to strike back if necessary. Your pupils dilate to take in as much visual information as possible, your stress hormones start converting fuel into energy, and your immune system helps ensure that these stress reactions don't harm your body in the process of protecting it.

The sum of these activities is an increase in your overall energy . . . and that's useful when you've invaded the space of a large and powerful dog. The increased energy from your body's stress reaction helps prepare you for a *fight-or-flight* response: You try either to fight off an attack by yelling at the dog and scaring it away or to remove yourself hastily from the scene. Each strategy can help ensure your survival by reducing the chances of an attack or minimizing the damage caused by one. (Even if you aren't *likely* to die from a dog attack, such an outcome is possible, and it is the job of the stress response to diminish that possibility.)

That's an example of how stress is supposed to work. When you encounter some type of threat to your well-being, your body reacts by increasing your energy so that you can respond to the threat successfully. Some threats are physical in nature, such as encountering a growling dog or facing a serious illness. Threats can also be social (such as being embarrassed in front of your friends), emotional (such as losing a loved one), or economic (such as being laid off from work). In each of these situations, your mind perceives a potential for harm and initiates your body's stress reaction.

Did You Know?

Stress has an upside as well as a downside. Despite feeling unpleasant, stress can improve our resilience and can even increase our creativity.

To be effective, though, the strength of your stress response needs to be within a certain range. If you don't experience *enough stress* in reaction to a threat, you may not be sufficiently motivated—or sufficiently enabled—to respond to it. That leaves you more vulnerable to being harmed. Without the spike in your energy and attentiveness, for instance, you'd be less able to ward off an attack from the German shepherd you encountered on your walk, increasing your odds for injury. When we think about stress in that way, we quickly realize how critical it is to our survival and well-being.

Some of our bodies are indeed unable to mount an adequate stress response . . . but the more common problem is that we experience *too much stress*. That means that when we encounter stressors, our bodies overreact, producing a greater stress response than the threat warrants. Suppose you come upon a garter snake during your evening walk instead of a dog. Many people fear snakes, so encountering one—even a harmless one—causes some level of stress reaction in many of us. It would not be good if the harmless garter snake caused you the same level of stress as the snarling German shepherd poised to attack, though. If it did, that would be an overreaction—and when the body overreacts to a threat, it ends up harming itself in the process.

So there is what we might call a Goldilocks zone when it comes to stress: We want our stress response to be *not too weak, not too strong, but just right.* Let's return to our observation that the more affectionate people are, the less likely they are to overreact to stressors. When we stress out research participants after measuring their trait affection levels, we find that highly affectionate people have smaller increases in their cortisol and heart rate, compared to less-affectionate people. The stress reactions of affectionate people are strong enough to be adequate, but they are less likely to be too strong, which helps their bodies respond to stressful situations properly.

That finding illustrates what psychologists call a *stress-buffering effect.* The idea is that having close, affectionate relationships acts as a buffer—a protection—against life stressors. Over the years, several studies have found that the more affection and support people have in their lives, the less their bodies react to stressful events.

The Impact of Oxytocin

We have known for a while that affectionate people react less to stressors than non-affectionate people, but we haven't really known what in the body causes that difference. In a recent study, however, communication professors Colin Hesse and Perry Pauley and I explored the possibility that the stress-buffering effect of trait affection is related to the hormone oxytocin.

Ask Yourself

In what ways do your close relationships help to protect you from stressful events?

Oxytocin is a feel-good hormone that is elevated by sexual orgasm and even by affectionate nonsexual touch, such as a back rub. Many pop psychology enthusiasts have dubbed oxytocin the "love hormone." One of the many things it does to the body is to suppress activity in the HPA axis, which is the system responsible for churning out cortisol when we feel stressed. In that way, oxytocin plays a part in helping us avoid overreacting to stressful events. Remember that you want your stress responses to be in that Goldilocks zone, not too weak and not too strong. It appears that oxytocin helps to rein in the stress response so that it isn't overly strong and needlessly damaging to the body.

To find out if that was indeed the case, we conducted another one of our stress experiments, subjecting more brave volunteers to our stressful activities after having reported on their trait affection levels. This time, though, we took blood samples at various points during the stressful events to monitor their oxytocin. As we expected, people's levels of trait affection were related to their changes in oxytocin: The more affectionate they were, the more their oxytocin increased when they were stressed out. Because oxytocin alleviates pain, imparts feelings of pleasure, and reins in the stress response, it serves as a form of protection against stressful situations—and highly affectionate people get more of this protection than their non-affectionate counterparts do.

The physical health benefits associated with trait affection are especially evident during instances of stress, but they aren't limited to those instances. In various ways, highly affectionate people are simply healthier than less-affectionate people are, even when differences in age, diet, exercise, sleep patterns, and body size are taken into account. For example, our research shows that affectionate people have:

- Lower resting blood pressure and lower resting heart rates than do less-affectionate people.
- Lower average blood sugar levels, which is significant because blood sugar is elevated by stress.
- Stronger immune systems, insofar as their natural killer cells—cells that attack virally infected cells and malignant growths in the body—are more efficient and more effective than are those of less-affectionate communicators.

Clearly, there are mental and physical health benefits associated with being an affectionate person. Of course, any of us can find ourselves in a *state* of behaving affectionately, even if our *trait* level of affectionate communication isn't especially high. Just like the hug I received outside my office on a distressing morning, sharing affection during times of stress—regardless of our trait levels of affectionate behavior—does a lot to help our bodies. Let's discover how in the next section.

Expressing Affection Is Healthy, Regardless of How Affectionate You Normally Are

Having a high score on the Trait Affection Scale is associated with many benefits, which is great news unless your own score is on the low end. You may not be a particularly affectionate person; maybe that simply isn't who you are. Even so, you probably give or receive affection from time to time. Perhaps you share hugs at meaningful events, such as weddings and graduations. Maybe you're affectionate with people you haven't seen in a long while. Most of us engage in affectionate behavior on occasion, even if we don't do so regularly.

According to research, sharing affection is beneficial even if it's uncommon for us. The health benefits of engaging in affectionate behavior—regardless of your trait affection level—are most pronounced when you are anticipating, experiencing, or recovering from a stressful event. Studies show that sharing affectionate behavior with someone has one of two effects on the body:

1. If the affection occurs *prior to* a stressful event, the body is protected against overreacting (i.e., a buffering effect).
2. If it happens *after* exposure to the stressor, the body returns to its normal level of functioning more quickly (a recovery effect).

You'll recall my earlier description of our research that involved deliberately stressing people out, in order to see how the body responds. Studies of the buffering and recovery effects typically use the same kind of design: There is some activity intended to elevate stress. The difference is that participants share affection with someone (verbally or nonverbally) either right before the stressful activities or immediately afterward. In either case, the body benefits.

Affection Is Helpful Just Before a Stressful Event

The doctor of philosophy degree, or PhD, is the highest academic degree a person can earn in most fields of study. PhD programs are typically three to five years in length and nearly always culminate in a massive research project known as a dissertation. To complete their programs, students must not only *write* a dissertation but also *defend* it in front of a committee of professors. Many years of work, expense, emotional turmoil, and delayed gratification follow students into their dissertation defense meetings, the outcome of which determines whether they pass their doctoral programs and receive the PhD or fail and go back to the drawing board.

Because the stakes are so high, the dissertation defense meeting is often enormously stressful for students. Mine certainly was. Partly to share their joy—and partly to help them get through without having an emotional breakdown—many PhD students bring spouses, relatives, close friends, and other significant people with them to their meetings. Guests sometimes have to wait outside while the defense occurs, but my observation is that they usually shower the student with affection beforehand. There are hugs, kisses, pats on the back, and reminders that "we love you," all of which the student usually soaks in before facing his or her doctoral committee. Does sharing affection before a stressful event—as this example illustrates—actually help us manage that stressor?

Erika's Story

ERIKA WAS ONLY THIRTY-SEVEN YEARS OLD WHEN SHE WAS DIAGNOSED WITH OVARIAN CANCER. AFTER UNDERGOING SURGERY,

SHE BEGAN AN AGGRESSIVE ROUND OF CHEMOTHERAPY. HAVING WATCHED HER AUNT ENDURE CHEMOTHERAPY AFTER A DOUBLE MASTECTOMY SEVERAL YEARS EARLIER, ERIKA KNEW THE TREATMENTS WOULD BE BOTH PHYSICALLY AND EMOTIONALLY TAXING. SHE THEREFORE DECIDED THAT BEFORE EACH TREATMENT, SHE WOULD SPEND TIME CUDDLING AND SHARING AFFECTION WITH HER HUSBAND, HER THREE YOUNG CHILDREN, AND HER CHERISHED BEAGLE. ALTHOUGH EACH ROUND OF THERAPY WAS STRESSFUL, ERIKA DISCOVERED THAT SHARING AFFECTIONATE TIME WITH HER FAMILY BEFOREHAND GAVE HER STRENGTH AND MADE EACH SESSION SEEM LESS DAUNTING.

Several studies suggest that sharing affection before encountering a stressor protects us from overreacting to it, just as Erika discovered. In one project, researchers at the University of North Carolina asked adults to hold hands for ten minutes with their romantic partners while viewing a romantic video, and then to share a twenty-second hug, all before going through a stress-inducing laboratory exercise (similar to the ones we use in my lab). A separate group of adults simply rested, quietly and alone, prior to the stressful activity. Compared to the participants who rested alone, those who shared affection with a loved one had lower increases in their heart rate and blood pressure during the stressful activity. In other words, their reaction to the stressor was buffered by the affectionate contact they had immediately beforehand.

The North Carolina study was limited to romantic relationships, but the stress-buffering effects of affection are not. In my lab, professors Perry Pauley and Colin Hesse and I repeated the North Carolina study but included pairs of both romantic partners and friends. Once again, people who shared affectionate behavior with someone before encountering stressful events had lower increases in heart rate and blood pressure than did people who sat quietly beforehand, either alone or in the company of their companion. The type of relationship participants had with their companion made no difference: Affection was equally effective at buffering stress when shared with a friend or a lover.

Is the type of relationship always inconsequential? Let's say that, before a stressful event, you held hands with a stranger, someone you didn't know at all. Would that buffer your body's stress reaction? At least one study suggests that it would. Psychologists James Coan, Hillary Schaefer, and Richard Davidson put married women inside an MRI machine that recorded images of their brains while the women anticipated receiving mild electric shocks. The anticipation of the shocks was the stressful event, and during this time, the women held hands either with their husband, an anonymous male experimenter, or no one.

The North Carolina study (and our later repetition of it) had already shown that holding hands with a romantic partner buffers the body's stress response, but this raises an important question: Is that buffering effect inherent in the behavior itself, or does it depend on the relationship in which it occurs? We might think that it's the behavior itself that provides the benefit. Given that people who simply sit quietly with their companions aren't similarly buffered from the effects of stress, we know it isn't just about *having someone there with you*; it's about *sharing affection with that person*. However, it's also logical to think that we would benefit more by sharing our affection with someone we actually cared about.

According to Coan and his colleagues, both ideas are true. In their study, holding hands with a husband *or* a stranger lowered women's activation in regions of the brain associated with stress and threat. However, the benefit was greatest when women held hands with their husbands. These results suggest that, in terms of stress buffering, some affection is better than no affection, and affection with a loved one is better than affection with a stranger.

Based on those findings, we could say it's better to get hugs, kisses, and pats on the back before a dissertation defense—or any stressful event—than not to get them at all. Those behaviors benefit us the most, however, when they come from people we love.

Affection Is Helpful Immediately after a Stressful Event

Recall my story about my horrible first day of summer school and the hug I received afterward from my friend. What's significant about that story is that such a brief gesture—a hug—helped me feel immensely better, even though it changed nothing that had happened to me before that.

You can probably think of occasions when receiving a hug, a touch, or a kind word helped you feel better after going through something stressful. Perhaps those gestures make you feel better emotionally because they remind you that you aren't alone—that you have someone close to you who supports you. In such situations, affection does more than help you emotionally, though; it also helps you physically by accelerating your body's recovery from stress.

Remember, when we face potential threats, stress is a very useful reaction for our bodies to have, so long as our stress response is within a certain range. Whatever the strength of our stress response, however, it's also best if we recover from it relatively quickly after the threat has passed. We don't want to stay stressed for longer than we need to, because our bodies end up damaging themselves in the process. Once the threat—the speech we have to give, the argument we're having with our boss, our worry about the medical test results we're anticipating—is over, it's best if our bodies return to their normal state as quickly as possible.

One reason sharing affection after a stressful event makes us feel good is that it accelerates our stress recovery, according to research. We first demonstrated this effect in my lab when, after stressing out our study participants, we assigned them to one of three groups:

1. Participants assigned to the *affection group* were asked to think of someone they loved and to write a letter to that person. We asked them to describe in their letters how much they cared about the person and why he or she meant so much to them, and we told them that they could send their letter if they wanted to, but they were not required to.

2. Participants in the *thought group* were also asked to think of someone they loved, but instead of writing to that person, they simply sat quietly and reflected on why they cared about that person so much.

3. Finally, participants in the *rest group* were instructed only to sit quietly and rest. Everyone in the study either wrote, thought, or rested for twenty minutes after being stressed out—and during that time, we monitored changes in their stress levels.

Who recovered from their stress the fastest? You might think it was those who sat quietly and rested—but as you've probably experienced, your mind can keep a stressful experience alive even if your body is trying to recover. It's easy to sit and stew about something mentally, which tends to keep things like our blood pressure and cortisol levels high. Instead, the people who wrote "love letters" recovered much faster than the sit-and-resters. Their bodies returned to their normal, pre-stressed state at an accelerated rate, compared to people who rested quietly.

Did You Know?

For women, sharing physical affection with a partner on one day predicts less stress and a more positive mood on the following day.

Here's the tricky question, though: Was it *thinking about* their loved ones that sped up their stress recovery, or was it *putting their thoughts into words* that did it? Many of us feel good—perhaps even feel better after a stressful event—when we think of the people who matter to us, so it's possible that the love letter group recovered faster not because they were composing affectionate messages but simply because they had their loved ones on their minds. Resolving that quandary was the purpose of the thought group: If they also recovered from their stress faster than the sit-and-resters, then that points to *thinking about love* rather than *expressing love* as the beneficial act.

The answer is that simply thinking about loved ones (but not writing to them) was no more beneficial than doing nothing. People in the thought group and the rest group recovered from stress at the same rate—it was only those in the affectionate writing group who showed accelerated recovery.

We can conclude from that study that there is something special about *conveying* your feelings of affection—through words, in this case—that speeds recovery from stress. Merely feeling the feelings doesn't do it: It's the act of expressing those feelings that matters.

Take Matters Into Your Own Hands

These experiments show that sharing affection in the wake of stress encourages recovery, but there's another, subtler lesson here. When you find yourself feeling distressed, it's not necessary to wait for others to show affection to you. Rather, you can accelerate your own recovery by communicating affection to others. Instead of waiting for a hug, give a hug . . . or make a phone call, or write a love letter. When you receive *or* express feelings of affection with people you care about, you help return your body to a calm, non-stressed state as efficiently as possible.

It is difficult to exaggerate how significant affection is to the human experience, so it should come as little surprise that sharing affection contributes to our physical health and mental well-being. Are you deprived of affection in your own life? Continue on to the next chapter to assess your own level of affection hunger and to see how you compare with others.

Stop and Reflect

In this chapter, we have seen that affection—whether considered as a state or a trait—is healthy, particularly because it helps us manage stress. Before proceeding to Chapter Four, consider these questions and take note of how you would respond:

- Were you surprised at all to learn your trait affection level? Was it higher or lower than you expected? If so, how does this change the way you see yourself and your relationships, if at all?
- Consider your trait level of affection. When do you tend to express more affection than usual? Under what circumstances do you become less affectionate?
- How can you use affection to manage stress more efficiently in your life?

PART TWO

How Affection Hungry Are You?

Our task in Part Two is to diagnose your own affection hunger. We'll also identify the mistakes people make when treating their loneliness and the self-destructive ways in which they often cope with it. Chapter Four, Affection Hunger and You, helps you identify whether you are at low, moderate, or high risk of affection deprivation, and explains how your score compares to the score of people like you. In Chapter Five, Living in an Affection Famine, we explore the numerous ways in which social disconnection harms us mentally, emotionally, and physically. Finally, Chapter Six, The Misguided Paths We Follow, explains some of the common mistakes people make when trying to attract more social connection in their lives, and it identifies several coping strategies that do more harm than good.

CHAPTER FOUR

Affection Hunger and You

Imagine for a moment that an unthinkably ferocious tropical storm is obliterating your hometown. As wind speeds approach 175 miles per hour, violent storm surges flood your city, burying homes, roads, and everything else under a blanket of water. Everything you need to get by—food, shelter, medicine, drinking water, electricity—is being wiped out, and during one of the hottest months of the year. To make matters worse, the local and state authorities you count on to keep you safe don't seem to be doing much of anything to help.

In that distressed state, how many people in your life could you *count on* to come forward and help you?

That's a question many Hurricane Katrina survivors must have pondered. When the hurricane—one of the five deadliest in U.S. history—slammed the city of New Orleans in August 2005, it left tens of thousands in a state of despair, lacking many of the basic necessities for survival. Perhaps you still remember the aerial news photos of survivors trapped on their rooftops, surrounded by floodwater, unable to escape and desperate for rescue. Had they forgotten that their mayor ordered a mandatory evacuation from the city only days before? Why, then, were they still there and now trapped, their very lives at stake?

In the days that followed Katrina, most everyone had an opinion as to why some residents escaped to safety while others did not. Perhaps it was municipal corruption, an unfortunate but longstanding tradition in New Orleans government, that stalled the implementation of evacuation plans. The Federal Emergency Management Agency (FEMA) certainly shares some of the blame, as does perhaps the Louisiana governor's office. Then there's the charge of racism—white people were rescued while black people were left behind—that permeated the discussion. There's also the counter-observation that survival depended more on wealth than on ethnicity, insofar as rich African Americans fared better than poor white people.

I still wonder about the folks trapped on their rooftops, though. Maybe they were there because they were poor, or because they were minorities, or because their government was inept, corrupt, or both. If they had evacuated the city as the mayor ordered, however, they wouldn't have been stuck in the first place. Is it possible that those unfortunate people simply didn't have anyone they could count on to help them out? Is it conceivable that when the evacuation order was made, those folks had no one they could call—not a relative, a friend, or anybody—who would ensure that they got out safely? *No one?*

That may sound unlikely, but I don't think it actually is. Take stock of your own social circle for a moment. It's true that most of us haven't had to contend with a massive hurricane. Hopefully you've never faced anything remotely as devastating, when your very survival depended on having someone who could help you.

Instead, just think about whom you can talk to. When something important is happening in your life, do you have someone you can tell? Consider just the past six months: Whom do you talk to about your life?

Researchers asked several thousand Americans that question in 1985 as part of the General Social Survey, a wide-scale sociological study sponsored by the National Science Foundation. Back then, nine out of ten Americans named at least one confidant, someone with whom they could share the important matters in their lives. Only the remaining 10 percent said they had nobody to talk to. Two decades later, in 2006, sociologists asked the question again. This time, however, the results pointed to a troubling trend: Americans were becoming substantially lonelier. When asked whom they could talk to about important matters, fully 25 percent of people said "no one."

That's one in four Americans—nearly 80 million people—who can't name a single person they can talk to about the important issues in their lives. How many more would say they'd have no one to help them cope with a natural disaster?

As a people, we Americans are famished for genuine human connection. Perhaps that's how you feel—and if it is, you're certainly not alone. Before you can treat problems such as loneliness and affection hunger, though, you need to diagnose the condition in yourself, which we'll do next.

How Affection Deprived Are You?

We all have occasions when we feel lonely or isolated, without the affection and intimacy we want or need. Experiencing affection deprivation now and then is normal—and it's not usually a problem, because we eventually return to a state in which our affection needs are met. The problem occurs when we are *chronically* affection deprived. How well does that condition describe you? Read and respond to the items in the "Ask Yourself" box to find out.

Ask Yourself

Consider how much you agree or disagree with each of the following statements by assigning it a number between 1 and 7. Assign a higher number if you agree more, and a lower number if you agree less.

1. One thing I would change about my close relationships is to receive more affection.
2. I frequently wish for more affection than I get.
3. I don't get enough affection in my life.
4. I wish the people in my life would hug me more often.
5. Affection is something I could use more of in my life.
6. I rarely receive as much affection from others as I want.
7. In general, I feel like I am affection deprived.
8. I wish my loved ones would express their love for me more often.

Once you've assigned a number between one and seven to each item, add your numbers together. Your total score should be between 8 and 56.

(These items were originally published in Floyd, K. (2014). Relational and health correlates of affection deprivation. *Western Journal of Communication* 78: 383–403. Reproduced with permission.)

The items in the "Ask Yourself" box come from a scale called the Affection Deprivation Index, which is used in research to measure people's experiences of chronic affection deprivation. In fact, it has been used in several of the studies I describe in this book. Let's consider what your score means.

Diagnosing Yourself

If you scored from 8 to 23, then you are at **low risk** of chronic affection deprivation. You may have many close relationships in your life or only a few. In either case, you usually feel that you receive adequate affection from the people you care about. Although you may have occasions when you wish for more affection than you get, those occasions are infrequent and do not cause you sustained distress.

If you scored from 24 to 40, then you are at **moderate risk** of chronic affection deprivation. Whether you are close to many people or have only a few intimate relationships, you find yourself on a somewhat frequent basis wishing for more affection than you actually receive. You appreciate the people in your life and you realize they care about you, but you would prefer that they express their affection for you a bit more. The gap between the affection you want and the affection you get is big enough that you notice it, but the distress it causes you is only moderate, not substantial.

If you scored from 41 to 56, then you are at **high risk** of chronic affection deprivation. If you had your way, your romantic partner and/or your close friends and relatives would be significantly more affectionate with you than they are. You might have one close relationship that is adequately affectionate but desire more affection from others in your life—or, you may feel there is no one in your life who really meets your affection needs. In either case, your lack of affection may frequently weigh heavily on your mind. Even if you have many people in your life, you likely feel lonely and that there is no one who really "gets" you. You may also feel depressed; if not all the time, then often.

These are general descriptions of the three levels of scores—low, moderate, and high risk—and yours may not describe you perfectly. There are many ways to experience affection deprivation (if we face it at all), and no two people's experiences are exactly alike. Whether your score came out as you expected or was more of a surprise, these descriptors illustrate in broad terms what is often true of others with your level of risk.

How Your Score Compares

When making sense of your score, it's useful to know how you compare to other people who are similar to you. Consider your biological sex, for instance. As the following figure shows, scores indicating moderate risk are most common for both women and men, although men are more likely than women to have moderate risk. Men are also slightly more likely than women to have high risk. On the contrary, however, women are more likely than men to have low risk. As we'll discover, men typically score higher than women do on the affection deprivation scale, and these results reflect that difference.

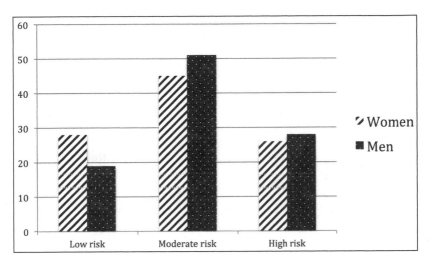

Percentages of women and men scoring at low, moderate, and high risk for chronic affection deprivation

Now consider your racial or ethnic background. As the following figure shows, scores indicating moderate risk are once again more common than scores reflecting high or low risk, but there is some variation among ethnic groups. For instance, Asians are the most likely to have moderate risk and the least likely to have low risk. Hispanics are the most likely to have low risk (followed closely by African Americans), and Caucasians are the most likely to have high risk.

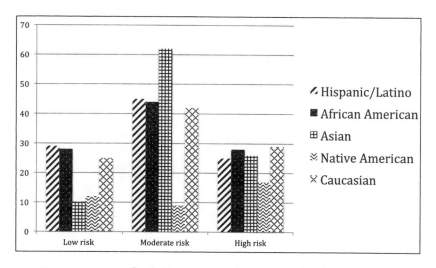

Percentages of ethnic groups scoring at low, moderate, and high risk for chronic affection deprivation

Considering your score in light of your own sex and ethnicity allows you to see how you compare to those who are similar to you on these factors. As our focus in this book is primarily on people experiencing loneliness, though, let's delve more deeply into the characteristics of those at high risk for chronic deprivation. What kind of individual tends to be highly affection deprived?

People around the world have completed the Affection Deprivation Index. Looking across those data offers us information as to who a highly affection-deprived person is. There are always exceptions to the rule, of course—virtually anyone *can* feel lonely and deprived of affection. From the research, however, we can say that highly affection-deprived people tend to:

- *Be male.* Most studies that have used the Affection Deprivation Index (although not all) have found that men score higher, on average, than do women.
- *Be single or divorced.* Adults who are single (never married) and those who are divorced score higher on affection deprivation than those who are married and those who are widowed.
- *Live in Germany.* Across all the countries in which affection deprivation has been measured, Germany scores the highest.
- *Live on the coast.* For those in the United States, people living on either the West Coast or the East Coast score highest in affection deprivation.
- *Be Asian American.* When we consider raw scores on the affection deprivation scale, instead of clustering people into categories, we find that, among Americans, those who claim an Asian background report higher levels of affection deprivation than those with other ethnic backgrounds.
- *Make more money.* The higher a person's total household income (from all sources), the more affection deprived he or she tends to be.
- *Have a mental illness.* Affection-deprived adults are more likely to have been diagnosed with an anxiety disorder (such as panic disorder, social phobia, obsessive-compulsive disorder, or post-traumatic stress disorder) and/or a mood disorder (such as depression, bipolar disorder, or substance-induced mood disorder).
- *Be neurotic.* Neuroticism is a personality trait that describes someone's tendency toward anxiety, moodiness, jealousy,

and worry. People who feel deprived of affection also tend to have neurotic personalities.

- *Have no one to turn to.* Like many of those caught in Hurricane Katrina, affection-deprived people are far more likely to say they have no one in their lives whom they can turn to in times of need.

Not all of a person's characteristics influence his or her affection-deprivation levels, of course. For instance, affection hunger has virtually no relationship with a person's age, height, weight, education level, or number of children.

Breaking Down the Data

If we were to identify a prototype of the highly affection-deprived American from these comparisons, it would be a divorced Asian American man living on the coast who makes good money, has a neurotic personality, and suffers from an anxiety and/or mood disorder. We can say with some confidence that such a man—if he exists in real life—would likely feel that he rarely gets as much affection as he wants. Importantly, though, we can't determine from these comparisons whether any of these attributes *causes* someone to be affection deprived. For example, divorced people feel more deprived than married people, but that doesn't necessarily mean that getting divorced causes affection deprivation. It is at least equally likely that feeling affection deprived increases your odds of getting divorced. By the same token, affection-deprived people are more likely to have mood or anxiety disorders, but that doesn't prove that having such a disorder causes someone to be affection deprived. These are simply comparisons between groups, not necessarily cause-and-effect relationships.

When it comes to social behaviors such as affection, characteristics like income level or neuroticism sometimes make a difference, but often they do not. Of all the ways in which people vary, however, two that frequently influence our social behaviors are our sex and our cultural background. Let's look at bit more closely at how they relate to affection hunger.

Sex and Culture in Affection Deprivation

Most of us recognize that women and men—as well as people in various cultural groups—are different, so it probably comes as little surprise to find sex and cultural differences in affection deprivation. What accounts for those differences, though? When it comes to feeling affection deprived, why do sex and culture matter?

The Sexes Differ in Affection Deprivation

On average, men feel slightly more affection deprived than women do. (The sex difference isn't large; men score on average only two points higher than women do. That's a larger difference than we would expect to see by chance alone—but not by very much. So we want to be careful not to make too big a deal of it.) Why do you suppose that's true? I think two scenarios, in particular, are worth considering. Remember that the very concept of *deprivation* implies wanting or needing more of something than we receive. That gives rise to two possibilities for why men feel more affection deprived than women:

1. It may be the case that women and men receive the same amount of affection from others, but men simply want more affection than women do, causing men to feel more deprived.

2. On the contrary, it could be that women and men want the same amount of affection, but women receive more of their desired affection than men do, which would also lead men to feel more deprived.

Either of these scenarios is possible, but they cannot both be true . . . so which is it? According to research, it's the second one. On average, *women and men want the same amount of affection from others.* That doesn't necessarily mean they want affection from the same people, or in the same forms, or at the same times . . . they simply prefer the same amount overall. I don't find that particularly surprising, any more than I'd be surprised to learn that women and men want the same amount of sleep, water, or oxygen. Obviously there's variation from person to person—every individual woman doesn't want the same amount of affection, nor does every individual man. When you simply compare the averages of what women and men want, however, you find they're the same.

Gene's Story

LIKE MANY OTHER MEN IN THEIR LATE SIXTIES, GENE HAS HAD A FULL AND BUSY LIFE. HE AND HIS WIFE ELEANOR HAVE RAISED THREE CHILDREN, EACH OF WHOM IS NOW MARRIED WITH CHILDREN OF THEIR OWN. HE RECENTLY RETIRED AFTER A LONG CAREER IN ENGINEERING, AND NOW HE AND ELEANOR SPEND MORE OF THEIR TIME ALONE TOGETHER THAN AT ANY OTHER POINT IN THEIR MARRIAGE. THEY HAVE ALWAYS BEEN MODERATELY AFFECTIONATE WITH EACH OTHER, BUT ELEANOR ALSO HAS MANY AFFECTIONATE FRIENDS FROM CHURCH THAT SHE SPENDS TIME WITH, WHEREAS GENE'S FREE TIME IS SPENT WORKING ALONE IN HIS YARD OR GARAGE. ALTHOUGH HE WOULD NEVER DESCRIBE HIMSELF AS "AFFECTION DEPRIVED," GENE PRIVATELY LONGS FOR MORE AFFECTION THAN HE GETS.

Importantly, though, *women receive more affection than men do*, at least in North America. There are many possible explanations for that sex difference:

- It may be that people find women more approachable, more receptive to affection, or more appreciative of affectionate behavior than men.
- It could be that, like Eleanor and Gene, women are more likely than men to participate in social groups where affectionate behavior is common—for example, at church gatherings, hobby clubs, or in child care settings.
- It might also be the case that people *perceive* women to require more affection than men (even though they don't say they do), so they are more affectionate with women as a result.

Any of these explanations could account for this sex difference, but we don't yet know which explanation is correct. It may also be a combination of reasons. The important point, though, is that women and men want the same amount of affection, yet women receive more (for whatever reason), which is why men report greater deprivation.

Did You Know?

When evaluating the adjectives used to measure gender roles, 43 percent of people in one study considered "affectionate" to be a feminine trait, whereas 57 percent considered it a gender-neutral trait. None considered "affectionate" to be a masculine trait.

Cultures Differ in Affection Deprivation

Next to sex, culture is probably the most commonly studied influence on behavior, and for good reason. If you've ever traveled abroad—or interacted with visitors from another country—you know that people from different cultures engage the world in quite divergent ways. They may dress differently, speak differently, have different beliefs, eat different foods, communicate differently, and value different things. Indeed, if men are from Mars and women are from Venus—as John Gray's 1992 book suggested—then people from different cultures can seem like they're from other galaxies. As a result, it's not difficult to believe that cultural groups differ in their levels of loneliness and affection deprivation as well.

I've found that Germans score highest on affection deprivation. For researchers who study body language and other forms of nonverbal communication, Germany is an example of what is called a *low contact culture*, which I think helps to explain their affection deprivation. Not every German person is the same, of course—but compared to other populations, Germans as a group keep more personal space around themselves, and they tend not to touch each other very much, leading to the description of their culture as "low contact." There's an expectation in low contact cultures that personal space is respected, and that touch—at least in social settings—is minimal. Although people can express their affection through words, facial expressions, and other non-contact behaviors, many of the most potent affectionate behaviors involve touch, such as hugging, kissing, and handholding. If touch is limited by cultural mandate, as it is in low contact cultures such as Germany, then it's easy to understand why people might feel deprived of affection.

Here's an interesting twist, though: Number two on the list of affection-deprived cultures is Italy, which is a decidedly *high contact culture.* Unlike their German counterparts, Italians observe very little personal space, and they touch each other much more often. For instance, one observational study compared touch in public, social settings in Italy, the United States, and Germany. In male-female pairs, Italian adults were nearly four times as likely as German adults (and 8 percent more likely than American adults) to touch each other. In male-male pairs, Italians were nearly three times as likely as Germans and almost ten times as likely as Americans to touch. When the interactions were between two women, Italians were more than twice as likely as Americans to touch.

Considered together, these findings confirm what many tourists have discovered on their own: Compared to Germans and Americans, Italians are touchy-feely folks. That makes it somewhat puzzling that Italy trails only Germany in affection deprivation. Italians certainly hug, kiss, and share contact with each other much more than Germans do . . . but remember that deprivation is about the difference between *what we get* and *what we want or need.* Even though Italians receive more affection than Germans do, it's entirely possible that they also *want* more affection than Germans do—and that they want more than they get.

Ask Yourself

When you interact with people who are more touchy-feely than you—as people from some cultures tend to be—how do you feel? Do you find it uncomfortable, or do you enjoy their higher level of contact?

Following Italy and Germany in the list of the most affection-deprived countries are Canada, Australia, Bahrain, Togo, Andorra, Syria, India, and Singapore, all of which outscore the United States. Thus, although affection deprivation is a common problem among Americans, it appears to be even more common elsewhere in the world.

Did You Know?

Compared to teachers of other ethnic backgrounds, Hispanic teachers are perceived as more affectionate, more friendly, and more helpful, according to research.

Within the United States, affection deprivation is lowest in the South and in Hawaii. Although the Hawaiian and Southern cultures are markedly different, one attribute that these locations have in common is that they are warm. You may not necessarily think of weather as a contributing factor to affection deprivation, but years of research have actually shown a strong relationship between 1) how much people in a given culture touch each other, and 2) how close that cultural group is to the equator. The closer people are to the equator, the hotter their climates are and the higher contact their cultures are.

I remember being perplexed when I first learned of this relationship, as it seemed counterintuitive. Frankly, I would've thought that people in cold climates would touch each other more, if only because they needed the warmth. On top of that, I know that when I'm extremely hot and sweaty, touching others is the last thing I want to do. The prediction that climate affects touch behavior was actually advanced in the mid-1700s by a French philosopher with the unwieldy name of Charles-Louis de Secondat, Baron de La Brède et de Montesquieu. These days, we simply call him Montesquieu—and he surmised that the climate in which people live influences the type of personalities they develop. Specifically, he thought that people in cold climates develop icy, standoffish dispositions, whereas those in hot climates are hot-tempered and affiliative. (Perhaps self-servingly, he proposed that the ideal climate for the fostering of personality was that of his home country of France.)

For modern-day social scientists, the gist of Montesquieu's theory is that individuals in warm environments are more expressive overall, not just with touch but with all manner of body language and verbal communication. As an illustration, consider people from Mediterranean countries such as Greece, Italy, or Spain. You can easily picture them being quite expressive, using their voice, facial expressions, and gestures to communicate with others clearly and emphatically. In comparison, consider people from northern Alaska or Siberia. You would be accurate to picture them being much more reserved, on average, than their Mediterranean brothers and sisters. Why is this the case, though? Montesquieu argued that when bodies come into contact with cold, blood is drawn from the extremities into the core, and this has the effect of slowing movement as a means of conserving energy. Therefore, cold temperatures discourage people from wasting their strength by gesturing about or being more expressive than necessary. When warmth is abundant, however, bodies relax and have less of a need to conserve energy, allowing people to express emotions and attitudes more passionately.

Did You Know?

Even college students touch each other more in warmer climates. In a study of universities across the United States, communication experts Janis and Peter Andersen found that students touched each other the least at the University of Minnesota and the University of Washington, which are both located close to the northern U.S. border. On the contrary, students touched the most at San Diego State University and Arizona State University, both located near the southern border.

Affection: A Product of Nature and Nurture

In the previous chapter, you determined your trait affection level—that is, your typical "set point" when it comes to giving and receiving affection with others in your life. Now that you know where you stand, what can you do about it? Is your affection level set in stone, or can you change it?

As with many traits, both nature and nurture appear to play a role. Some traits—such as whether you have brown eyes, Type O blood, or sickle cell anemia—are the exclusive domain of nature. For those, one or more genes determine the outcome entirely. If you have a point mutation in the ß-globin chain of the hemoglobin molecule, you will develop sickle cell disease no matter how much money you make, how distant your father was, or how many Facebook friends you have. Environmental influences—that is, the effects of "nurture"—are similarly irrelevant to your eye color and blood type. For many physical traits and most psychological and behavioral traits, however, genetic inheritance and environmental conditions are both contributing factors. Consider, for instance, the trait of aggressiveness, wherein some people behave more aggressively than others. Research shows that approximately 44 percent of the variation in people's levels of aggressiveness is due to genetic characteristics inherited from their parents. The rest of the variation is due to aspects of their environment, which could include their economic status, their religion, or their level of exposure to media violence.

Affection Is Influenced by Nurture

Thus far, only a few studies have tackled the question of what accounts for a person's affection level. As with aggressiveness and other behavioral traits, both genetic and environmental effects appear to be influential. In one study, communication professor Mark Morman and I considered the possibility that people's affection levels are related to their parents' affection levels—that is, whether we learn to be affectionate by watching our folks. Our study examined that question in the context of men's relationships with their fathers. Plenty of research already suggests that boys who have loving, attentive fathers grow up to be loving men and attentive fathers themselves, so we reasoned that *some highly affectionate men would report having grown up with highly affectionate fathers*. In developmental psychology, this phenomenon is called *modeling*: that is, learning to behave in a certain way by observing our role models (such as our parents) behaving that way.

Craig's Story

WHEN HE AND HIS SISTER WERE YOUNG, CRAIG REMEMBERS THEIR DAD HUGGING AND KISSING THEM BOTH. ONCE CRAIG STARTED MIDDLE SCHOOL, THOUGH, HIS FATHER STOPPED BEING AFFECTIONATE WITH HIM, ALTHOUGH HE CONTINUED SHOWING AFFECTION TO CRAIG'S SISTER. CRAIG THINKS THAT WHEN HE BECAME A TEENAGER, HIS DAD STARTED THINKING OF HIM AS A MAN—AND HIS DAD HAS NEVER BEEN AFFECTIONATE WITH OTHER MEN. CRAIG NOTES THAT HIS FATHER HASN'T HUGGED HIM ONCE IN THE LAST THIRTY-FOUR YEARS, NOT EVEN AT HIS WEDDING. HE REALLY WANTS A MORE AFFECTIONATE RELATIONSHIP WITH HIS DAD—LIKE HE HAS NOW WITH HIS OWN SONS—BUT HE STRUGGLES TO MAKE THAT HAPPEN.

Professor Morman and I were also aware, though, that some people compensate for having uninvolved, emotionally distant parents by growing into warm, loving adults. The process of *compensation* means behaving in ways that are different—usually opposite from—those we observe in others. People raised by abusive parents, for instance, might resolve to be loving and nurturing toward their own children in order to make up for the abuses they suffered. We thought the same might be true for men and affection: Perhaps *some highly affectionate men would report having grown up with very non-affectionate fathers.*

We found both patterns in our study: The most affectionate dads were those who had either highly affectionate or non-affectionate fathers themselves. In other words, at least part of the variation in men's affection levels is attributable to the affection levels of their fathers. It is tempting to take this finding as evidence that affection patterns are learned—that is, transmitted from fathers to sons through observation. The ideas of modeling and compensation certainly make intuitive sense. If I grew up with an affectionate father, I would observe his affectionate ways and then learn to become affectionate myself, and if my dad were distant, I would observe his non-affectionate ways and then learn the reasons for being a more affectionate adult. Much of what we gain from our parents comes through learning. Whether through direct instruction or passive observation, our parents often teach us our first language, our religious and moral beliefs, our cultural practices, and a variety of life skills ranging from shoe tying to driving.

Affection Is Influenced by Nature, Too

Could there also be a genetic component to our trait affection level? Some recent evidence suggests that there is. In one study, communication professor Amanda Denes and I examined the influence of "rs53576," a variant on the oxytocin receptor gene. Oxytocin, you'll recall, has calming and pain-alleviating effects on the body. Like all hormones, through, it can affect only those organs and tissues that carry a receptor gene for it. Think of hormones as keys and receptor genes as keyholes. Just as a key can open a lock only if it fits the keyhole, hormones can work only where they find receptor genes specific to them.

Denes and I found that genetic variations on rs53576 are related to a person's trait affection level. However, it's reasonable to assume that a genetic effect on affection may be more influential in some social circumstances than in others. So many factors—including your level of trust in your close relationships—can influence how your affection levels play out in your life.

So what accounts for *your* trait affection level? It's impossible to answer that question completely, but we can say with some certainty that a combination of your genes, your social environment, and your personal experience is influential. Accounting for your affection level isn't a question of "nature *vs.* nurture," that is. Rather, it's an example of "nature *plus* nurture."

Affection is such an important need that we suffer in multiple ways when we don't get enough. As the next chapter explains, feeling lonely, socially disconnected, and affection deprived is associated with a wide variety of physical and mental problems.

Stop and Reflect

In this chapter, you were able to assess your own level of affection hunger and to understand how affection deprivation varies from person to person. Before moving on to Chapter Five, consider how you would respond to these questions:

- Suppose your romantic partner or best friend filled out the Affection Deprivation Index _for you_. Would that person evaluate you in the same way you evaluated yourself?
- In what ways do you notice your own cultural background and practices influencing your affectionate behavior with other people?
- To what extent do you think your own trait affection level is learned, as opposed to genetically determined?

CHAPTER FIVE

Living in an Affection Famine

Tehachapi is a Podunk town whose name most people can't pronounce. The small desert community southeast of Bakersfield, California, is known mostly for its wind farm and ostrich ranch. In other words, it's the kind of place where nothing very newsworthy ever happens. Except, that is, at Seth Walsh's house.

Life was never kind to Seth. He was a good-looking kid who had a warm smile, pronounced dimples, and deep, knowing eyes. In many ways, he was a typical thirteen-year-old who loved French fries and Pokémon. Still, he never really belonged. "He knew he was different," said his grandmother Judy. And when being different means being unaccepted, it can leave a teenager feeling like he has few options.

His family and most of his friends already knew he was gay, and they loved him anyway. His mannerisms and style of dress made him a frequent target for cruel teasing from his classmates, though. By the time he was in seventh grade, he was afraid to walk home from school, never knowing where he would get picked on next. Even at home, he'd be harassed on the phone and over the Internet. As his grandmother recalls, "He spent a lot of his life frightened."

In September 2010, Seth hanged himself in his backyard.

His mom, Wendy, found his nearly lifeless body suspended from a tree when she stepped outside to smoke. By the time the police arrived, he was unconscious and he had stopped breathing. Within thirty minutes, he was airlifted to a trauma center in Bakersfield where he remained unresponsive on life support for eight days before doctors declared him brain-dead. His mom made arrangements to donate his organs, and his family said good-bye.

Seth was far from alone in seeing suicide as a way to escape his pain. Earlier that very month, thirteen-year-old Asher Brown shot himself in the head with his stepfather's handgun, and fifteen-year-old Billy Lucas hanged himself from the rafters of his family's barn. And three days after Seth's suicide, Rutgers University freshman Tyler Clementi ended his life by jumping off the George Washington Bridge.

Seth, Asher, Billy, and Tyler never knew each other, but their short lives were tragically intertwined. All four boys had been teased, harassed, mocked, and made to feel less than equal by their peers because they didn't fit in. They'd been threatened and had their privacy violated. They were bullied, left out, ostracized, cut off from the social world around them.

They didn't belong, and so they left us way too soon.

It's tragic, no question. When anyone commits suicide, lives are shattered and communities are shaken. Even as you may feel for the families of those four boys—and those of thousands of others who end their own lives each year—you might also feel at a loss to understand what could drive someone to take such a drastic measure.

Some of us would explain Seth's suicide by appealing to the tremendous sense of angst he must have felt as a homosexual teenage boy growing up in a community that didn't embrace diversity. Indeed, recent news stories have told of gay adolescents in San Francisco—one of the gay-friendliest cities on Earth—being bullied for their sexual orientation. How much more do we imagine someone in a typical U.S. town has to endure on a daily basis? As most of us can well recall, the adolescent years already bring enough anxiety over fitting in without having the added burden of being gay.

Others of us might suspect that Seth was in poor mental health, even though that wasn't outwardly apparent. It is true that most people who die by suicide suffer from some form of mental illness at the time of their death, and that some mental illnesses have symptoms that can be overlooked and go undiagnosed for years.

Whether springing from normal angst or pathological distress, Seth's suicide was certainly encouraged by his failure to fit in. He wasn't like everyone else, and he knew it. More important, everyone else knew it as well. But why would not fitting in drive someone to take his own life? *So you're different,* you might be thinking: *So what?*

If you're different, be different.

That's a fair enough point. Many of us grew up being taunted about one characteristic or another. Glasses, braces, red hair, an unusual religion, a different skin color—we might have been teased for sticking out, especially during adolescence, when blending in is so valued. You survived it, and so did I. And with the benefit of time and the magic of maturity, we came to learn that it's our differences that make us individuals. The shy girl in glasses became an innovative school principal. The kid with the hearing aid is now in the state legislature. The boy who endured teasing for his braces is a loving dad with an extra dose of empathy to share with his sons. Rather than limit us, our differences simply set us on different paths toward becoming whoever we were going to be.

In other words, we learned to accept ourselves for who we are, despite what other people think. We realized that superficial differences don't matter in the grand scheme. If only those boys—Seth, Asher, Billy, and Tyler—could have made it through their own adolescence, they might have emerged with the same wisdom all the rest of us did: Living a full life is all about embracing our diversity.

While we're congratulating ourselves on knowing more about life than a thirteen-year-old boy, let me point out the following: You and I are full of crap. We can believe all we want that we've outgrown our adolescent need to fit in. We can sing along with Lady Gaga about being beautiful in our way. We can fancy ourselves independent voters and talk smugly about taking the road less traveled by.

Those may be comforting delusions, but delusions they are. Whether we choose to admit it, the truth is that each of us strives to fit in, not to stand out. We need to belong, not to roam free. Seth Walsh didn't just want affection and love from others, he needed it . . . and so does every one of us. As I've already explained, that need is a fundamental and hardwired aspect of the human experience. And as I'll detail in this chapter, failing to get the love and affection we need from others corresponds to a wide range of problems related to our physical health, mental health, cognitive abilities, and personal relationships.

Did You Know?

Lesbian, gay, bisexual, and transgender adolescents are far more likely than their straight peers to think about and attempt suicide, according to research.

To understand the problems that go along with affection hunger, it's useful to look beyond my own research on the topic and also include research on similar experiences. In particular, social exclusion and loneliness have been extensively studied for their negative effects, and those results are valuable to consider. Affection hunger doesn't require being socially excluded, of course, and it isn't *exactly* the same thing as loneliness. All of these states are similar, however, in that they involve a *deficit* in our desired amount of personal contact and connection with others. Therefore, we can learn some important lessons about affection deprivation by also considering what we know about loneliness and social exclusion. In this chapter, I will draw from research on all three topics.

Tina's Story

TINA GREW UP AS ONE OF FOUR GIRLS IN A CLOSE-KNIT TEXAS FAMILY. HER MOTHER, FATHER, AND SISTERS WERE ALL AFFECTIONATE AND EXPRESSIVE, AND IT WAS CLEAR THAT THEY CARED FOR EACH OTHER IMMENSELY. AFTER FINISHING COLLEGE, TINA LANDED AN EXCELLENT JOB IN MINNEAPOLIS, WHERE SHE HAS LIVED FOR NEARLY FOUR YEARS. ALTHOUGH SHE ENJOYS HER WORK, THE SEPARATION FROM HER FAMILY HAS BEEN HARD TO HANDLE. FOR MOST OF HER LIFE, SHE HAS BEEN SURROUNDED BY PEOPLE WHO FREELY EXPRESS THEIR

LOVE FOR HER, AND EVEN THOUGH SHE'S MADE A FEW FRIENDS FROM
WORK AND AT HER GYM, SHE FEELS FUNDAMENTALLY ALONE. AT TIMES,
IT SEEMS AS THOUGH SHE IS LITERALLY ACHING FOR AFFECTION.

Disconnection Physically Hurts

Perhaps the most evident problem associated with affection deprivation and social disconnection is that it hurts physically. To
understand why it would, let's consider why we experience pain
in the first place. Most of us don't enjoy feeling pain, yet we recognize that it serves a function. Specifically, pain is our body's way
of 1) alerting us that something is threatening our wellness, and
2) motivating us to take some sort of corrective action. Think of
what happens if you accidentally touch a hot burner on the stove.
You immediately feel pain (that's the alert) and you instantly
remove your hand from the burner (that's the corrective action).
You also avoid touching the burner again while it's still hot (which
is a preventative action). These are useful responses to an event—
touching a hot burner—that can quickly cause you tissue damage
and injury. In these and many other ways, pain serves as a built-in
alarm system alerting us to potential threats. Much as we may
long for a pain-free existence, the ability to feel pain is essential to
our survival.

Burning your hand on a hot stove produces physical pain, but
we also feel what scientists call *social pain*, which is the emotional
distress caused by events that thwart our need for social connection. This is the pain that Tina feels as a result of being isolated
from her family. If you have ever been rejected by the object of

your affection, felt excluded by friends or relatives, or discovered that your spouse has been unfaithful, then you know that these situations can all evoke intense feelings of hurt, agony, and despair. One can easily imagine Seth Walsh, Asher Brown, Billy Lucas, and Tyler Clementi enduring enormous social pain at the hands of those who mocked, bullied, and ostracized them.

In our minds, many of us distinguish physical pain and social pain as two different types of experience. Although we speak of having *heartache* or *hurt feelings*, we usually don't imply that those descriptors are literal. In other words, most of us can tell the difference between a broken bone and a broken heart. Despite our understanding, however, are social and physical pain actually different?

Evidence from the field of neuroscience suggests that they aren't as different as we once thought. On the contrary, physical and social pain appear to have a common neurological basis, each activating a structure near the middle of the brain called the anterior cingulate cortex, or ACC. Using imaging techniques to examine how the brain processes pain, research has demonstrated that experiences such as loneliness, ostracism, and social exclusion literally hurt.

Many such studies use an innovative online computer game called *Cyberball* to induce feelings of rejection. Here's how it works. You're seated in front of a computer monitor showing drawings of three people, one of whom is holding a ball. That drawing represents you, and the others represent players who are online elsewhere . . . or so you are told. The game begins with you tossing a ball to one of the other players. That player tosses it to the third player, who tosses it back to you. You continue this pattern for a few minutes, as if you were in a grassy field playing a game of catch with two friends on a sunny afternoon. Shortly, however, the other players begin tossing the ball less often to you and more often between themselves. After a bit, they stop throwing you the ball altogether, tossing it only to each other as if they had decided to exclude you for some reason. Once that occurs, you remain excluded for the rest of the game.

You might have guessed by now that the other "players" in the game aren't real people. Rather, the *Cyberball* program is configured to exclude anyone who plays it after only a few minutes. (Although most research participants don't know this while they are playing the game, they are told the true nature of the program at the end of the study, so they don't leave thinking they have been genuinely ostracized.)

Even though the social exclusion in *Cyberball* is contrived, participants in these research projects feel genuinely put off by it. One study showed, in fact, that *Cyberball* exclusion lowered participants' self-esteem, their sense of belonging and personal control, even their tendency to see their own existence as meaningful. And surprisingly, it had these effects *even when participants were told* that the game was programmed to exclude them. Our need for connection is so great, that is, that we suffer even when a computer rejects us.

Did You Know?

According to one study, people's levels of belonging, personal control, self-esteem, and meaningful existence also suffered when they were excluded from a group text message.

The exclusion does more than reduce self-esteem . . . it also causes pain. Using neuroimaging procedures, researchers have found that *Cyberball* exclusion has the same types of effects on the brain (especially in the ACC) as physically painful events do. In other words, social rejection produces sensations of pain similar to those caused by physical injury. That matters because the experience of pain emanates from the brain; when you touch a hot stove, it's your brain—not your fingertips—that generates the painful sensations you feel. To the extent that your brain reacts similarly to physically and socially painful events, therefore, they will feel similar to you.

Although *Cyberball* is often used to stimulate feelings of exclusion, the pain of social disconnection isn't limited to *Cyberball* players. Recall the affection deprivation scale that you completed in the previous chapter. In a recent study involving adults from the United States and several foreign countries, I found that affection deprivation is significantly related to the experience of chronic pain as well. Feeling disconnected from others isn't associated only with momentary pain, that is; it is also correlated with the experience of ongoing pain, a condition afflicting millions of Americans.

Ask Yourself

When you feel social pain, what corrective actions do you take? What have you found to be the most helpful?

Given that social and physical pain are so alike, you might wonder whether similar interventions are effective for both. Perhaps you reach for a pain reliever such as ibuprofen or acetaminophen when you get a headache . . . but would it occur to you to use the same medication to treat the pain of loneliness? There's evidence that such an approach works. Participants in one study took either acetaminophen (the principal ingredient in Tylenol) or a harmless placebo on a daily basis for three weeks. Those taking the pain reliever reported feeling less social pain beginning on day nine of the study. A later experiment found that ibuprofen (the active ingredient in Advil and Motrin) produced similar improvements in social pain related to exclusion, although for women only.

Disconnection Can Contribute to Poor Health

As I've argued throughout this book, we humans are such intensely social beings that having close, satisfying relationships is a necessity without which we cannot thrive. That's an observation you can probably appreciate if you have ever gone through a period of extreme loneliness or isolation yourself. During that time, you never feel quite right, and that's partly because your body reacts to the lack of social connection as it would to the lack of anything essential. As a result, people who feel lonely or affection deprived are at increased risk of various health problems.

Sleep Disruptions

One such problem relates to the quantity and quality of sleep that people get. Psychologist John Cacioppo has suggested that social disconnection affects health in part because lonely, disconnected people don't get as much restorative sleep as others do. The problem isn't necessarily that lonely people can't fall asleep—it's that they don't *stay* asleep long enough to reap its important benefits. In one study, Cacioppo and his colleagues recruited young adults to spend a night in their clinical research center while their sleep efficiency and quantity were monitored. Before reporting for the study, the participants filled out measures of their loneliness, depression, and related conditions. After spending the night in the clinic, they also monitored their own sleep at home for five nights.

Cacioppo and his team found that the more lonely participants were, the less likely they were to stay asleep after falling asleep. In other words, lonely adults spent more time awake during the night after having fallen asleep. If you've ever had trouble staying asleep, you know that's a problem because it keeps you from entering the deep REM stages of sleep, which is when your body benefits the most. After such a night, it's hard to feel rested—and if you experience this pattern regularly, your body's defenses against illness are weakened. In line with these findings, my own research has found that people's scores on the Affection Deprivation Index—the scale you filled out in the previous chapter—are not related to their ability to fall asleep, but they are related to their ability to stay asleep through the night.

A Weaker Immune System

Social isolation can also correspond to weaknesses in the immune system. Your immune system functions to protect your body against the harmful effects of invaders, such as bacteria, parasites, and viruses. To fulfill its mission, it relies on a wide range of tools, some of which have been shown to be less effective among people who feel socially disconnected. For example, natural killer cells play a critical role in defending the body against cancer, and studies show that natural killer cells are less active in lonely adults. People with high levels of loneliness are also more susceptible to Epstein-Barr virus, the virus that causes mononucleosis (also known as "the kissing disease"). Most of us carry the Epstein-Barr virus in our bodies already, but the virus usually stays in an inactive state in which it doesn't cause us any problems. If you're particularly lonely, however, your immune system has to work harder to keep the virus in check.

Did You Know?

Highly affectionate people don't have *more* natural killer cells than their less-affectionate counterparts . . . but the ones they do have are more effective.

In addition to these effects of loneliness, affection-deprived people are also more likely to have been diagnosed with at least one secondary immune disorder. Disorders of the immune system come in two forms:

1. *Primary immune disorders,* which include such conditions such as leukocyte adhesion deficiency and herpes simplex encephalitis, are inherited genetically.
2. *Secondary immune disorders,* including such conditions as multiple myeloma and AIDS, are acquired as a result of exposure to specific environmental influences. This can include influences of the social environment as well as the physical environment, making secondary immune disorders potentially responsive to deficits in social connection.

It turns out that the more affection deprived people are, the more likely they are to have been diagnosed with a secondary immune disorder. In other words, affection deprivation is associated with poorer immune functioning—but of the type that is acquired, not inherited. This doesn't necessarily mean that affection hunger *causes* immune disorders, but it may affect a person's social experience in ways that increase their likelihood.

To illustrate how, let's think for a moment about AIDS. We know that AIDS is caused by the human immunodeficiency virus, or HIV. Common ways of contracting HIV include having unprotected sex and/or sharing drug needles with an infected person. Is either activity more probable for a socially disconnected individual than for someone who receives sufficient affection?

We might speculate that people who feel lonely and deprived of affection would cope with those feelings by seeking social contact in the most expedient ways possible, even if doing so puts their health at risk. Having casual sex with a stranger one meets online, for instance, provides at least a short-term experience of intimacy and touch. Likewise, sharing recreational drugs with others creates a short-term social opportunity that may otherwise be lacking in a person's life. Casual sex with strangers increases the odds of infection with HIV or other sexually transmitted diseases (especially given that people rarely know the sexual history of their random sexual partners), and recreational drug use exposes people to a range of medical and legal risks. These are potentially significant problems . . . but loneliness is a troublesome state, and it isn't much of a stretch to imagine that people who are intensely lonely would take such risks in order to feel some connection with others.

In fact, research supports that speculation. As I explain in more detail in the next chapter, some people cope with social disconnection, loneliness, and affection deprivation in very self-defeating ways. Those include having casual sex with strangers and using illicit intravenous drugs, both of which elevate the chances of contracting HIV and AIDS.

Some of the health problems we've discussed here are likely compounded by the fact that lonely, affection-deprived people have worse health-care habits than their socially connected counterparts, as we'll consider next.

Disconnection Reduces Self-Care

People who feel lonely and disconnected aren't just in poorer health than others—they also take worse care of themselves. Compared to people who feel socially engaged, lonely adults exercise less, drink more alcohol, are more likely to smoke, and eat more of their daily calories as fat, all of which help to create and exacerbate their health problems.

Together, studies on this topic reveal a noteworthy pattern: *When people feel deprived of meaningful connection with others, they don't take care of themselves as well as they should.* Poor habits, of course, may compound the physical health problems that go along with loneliness. Let's examine some of the poor health habits associated with social disconnection.

Lack of Adequate Exercise

Regular exercise has many health benefits, including maintaining a healthy weight, regulating cholesterol and blood sugar, boosting energy, and promoting better sleep. Research shows, however, that both loneliness and shyness discourage people from exercising. One study found that college students who were either highly shy or highly lonely were less likely than their peers to exercise at all—and those who did exercised less often. Unfortunately, the effect isn't limited to undergraduates. A later study with older adults (aged fifty to sixty-eight years) similarly found that lonelier participants exercised less frequently than their peers, and they were also more likely to quit exercising altogether. Not surprisingly, therefore, loneliness is a significant risk factor for several problems that go along with a sedentary lifestyle, including obesity and elevated cholesterol and blood pressure.

There are at least two possible reasons why social disconnection discourages exercise:

- Exercise is often a social activity; many people run, bike, swim, or work out with close friends or relatives, which may contribute to the enjoyment of exercise and which is harder to do when you don't feel connected to anyone.
- People who feel lonely or affection deprived may believe—consciously or subconsciously—that exercise is pointless because they have no one to stay in shape *for*.

Whatever the reasons, a lack of exercise often goes hand in hand with other poor health habits, and that is true for the socially disconnected as well.

Alcohol and Tobacco Abuse

If you think about stereotypical images of loneliness, one that probably comes to mind is someone sitting alone in a bar, "looking for love at the bottom of a glass." As with many stereotypes, this one contains some truth, as several studies have found a connection between social isolation and alcohol abuse. Not surprisingly, alcoholics as a group frequently score higher on measures of loneliness than other groups. Loneliness is also related to perceiving oneself as a problem drinker and experiencing negative health, relationship, and financial consequences from drinking. Moreover, lonely people are more likely to smoke, increasing their risks of respiratory problems, lung cancer, and heart disease.

Poor Eating Habits

Finally, feelings of social disconnection correspond to poorer eating habits. In particular, people who feel lonely and disconnected consume a higher percentage of their daily calories from fat. Although your body needs fats to function properly, they should not comprise the majority of your diet. In a healthy diet, approximately 25 to 35 percent of daily calories should come from fats, according to the American Heart Association. For young adults, research shows no relationship between feeling disconnected and consuming fat. The effect of disconnection appears in older adults. In a study of middle-aged Americans, psychologist John Cacioppo found that an overall average of 34 percent of their daily calories came from fat. That's across all participants—but unlike with young adults, loneliness made a difference. The middle-aged adults in the study who were least lonely received only 29 percent of their daily calories from fats. For those who were most lonely, however, it was 39 percent, which exceeds the recommended limit for a healthy diet.

Disconnection Impairs Mental Health

The problems of social disconnection aren't just physical. Many people find that their mental health also suffers from a lack of meaningful relationships. As we've seen, loneliness and social isolation are associated with pain—but pain isn't always physical. Many experience disconnection primarily as a threat to their mental and emotional wellness.

Lonely and affection-deprived people simply feel less well in a broad sense. Researchers sometimes use a survey instrument called the General Health Questionnaire to measure a person's overall mental well-being. The instrument includes such questions as *Have you recently lost much sleep over worry?* and *Do you feel constantly under strain?* Feeling under strain and losing sleep to worry are nonspecific symptoms—that is, they can go along with more than one mental health problem—but they do indicate that a person is under some level of general emotional distress.

I have administered the General Health Questionnaire to research participants along with the Affection Deprivation Index. Unsurprisingly, scores on the two scales are strongly related: The more deprived of affection people feel, the more likely they are to experience general signs of mental and emotional distress. This suggests a connection between mental health and affection hunger, but by itself it doesn't tell us much about the specific types of mental health problems an affection-deprived person is likely to experience.

Like physical health, mental health is complex. There are well over a dozen broad categories of mental illness, from depression and stress disorders to sleepwalking disorder, anorexia, gender identity disorder, narcissistic personality disorder, panic disorder, and autism. These are diverse conditions, but they all represent social, cognitive, or emotional impairment of some variety. We certainly wouldn't expect affection deprivation to correspond to every type of mental disorder, but its relationship to the General Health Questionnaire suggests that at least some mental illnesses are probably more common for lonely, affection-deprived people.

Depression

One obvious candidate, I think, is depression. Remember that humans are an intensely social species—we have a powerful need for social relationships. When people feel excluded or cut off from meaningful connection in their lives, it's easy to imagine that they experience sadness and depressed emotion. Think of Seth Walsh, for instance—then consider how you would feel if you were constantly being rejected, bullied, and threatened by people who are supposed to be your friends. What Seth went through was the very antithesis of social inclusion, and in a similar situation, many of us would experience the symptoms of depression, such as self-loathing, irritability, sad and negative thoughts, and feelings of hopelessness. In fact, research confirms that depression is more common among people who experience high levels of affection deprivation, loneliness, and social exclusion.

Does the experience of social disconnection *cause* depression? It's easy to imagine that it could. Victims of bullying or other forms of social exclusion are much more likely than non-victims to be depressed . . . so unless they were already depressed before the bullying began, it's probable that being bullied led to their depression. It's also possible that depression causes social disconnection. That's because when we're depressed, the last thing most of us want to do is be around others. Depression usually leads us to focus our energies inward, preferring to withdraw into solitude instead of engaging with people. We can therefore think of depression as both a cause and an effect of social deprivation.

In clinician-speak, depression is a form of mood disorder, a mental illness that primarily impairs a person's mood or affect. It often co-occurs with conditions called anxiety disorders, such as panic disorder, obsessive-compulsive disorder, post-traumatic stress disorder, and separation anxiety. This led me to wonder whether affection deprivation is related to the number of mood and anxiety disorders with which people have been diagnosed. In a survey of over 500 adults from the United States and a range of foreign countries, I administered the Affection Deprivation Index and then presented a list of mood and anxiety disorders, asking participants to indicate how many they had been diagnosed with (although I didn't ask them to specify which ones). As I expected, the more affection deprived people felt, the more mood and/or anxiety disorders they had.

Alexithymia

Deficits in mental health often impair our social and relational experiences, of course. Consider autism, which frequently impedes the development of language skills and limits a person's ability to understand social cues such as facial expressions. Although many people with autism have highly advanced memory or mathematical skills, their social abilities are often quite diminished.

A condition called *alexithymia* is similar in many ways to autism, except that it isn't considered a mental illness. Rather, alexithymia is a personality characteristic that impairs people's ability to understand and express their own emotions and to interpret emotional signals from others. As an example, think of the character Sheldon Cooper from the television comedy *The Big Bang Theory.* Although Sheldon is a certified genius, his social experiences are inhibited by his inability to interpret the emotional meaning in other people's facial expressions or tone of voice. He is frequently unaware of when others are upset, for instance, and he regularly misses clues to sarcasm.

Each of us is alexithymic to some extent, but approximately 10 percent of the population has a high enough level of alexithymia to impede their social relationships. Like depression, therefore, high alexithymia is a liability when it comes to meeting our needs for social connection—and according to research, higher levels of alexithymia correspond to more intense feelings of affection deprivation.

Disconnection Leads to Cognitive Problems

Even for those who don't suffer from a mental disease or disorder, social disconnection corresponds to some difficulties with cognitive processes. For example, it impairs people's ability to think intelligently. In a series of studies, psychologists primed some participants to feel socially excluded by telling them that their answers on a personality questionnaire made them statistically likely to "end up being alone" in life. Compared to participants who didn't receive the same prediction, those told to expect social exclusion attempted fewer questions on an IQ test and answered a higher percentage of questions incorrectly. They also performed worse on the reading comprehension and analytical portions of the Graduate Record Exam (GRE), a standardized test required for admission to most graduate schools in the United States.

The people who were told they would end up alone in life were no less intelligent than the others in the study, yet they performed more poorly on virtually every cognitive task they were presented with. One possible explanation for this difference is that loneliness impairs a person's ability to concentrate. Especially when presented with novel experiences, lonely people work less hard to stay focused and on track, according to research. As a consequence, they may be less likely to pay attention, particularly when confronted with exam questions they haven't encountered before.

Being told to expect social exclusion doesn't just impair people's ability to concentrate. It also leads them to give up more easily when faced with a challenging task. In one study, people were asked to trace a complex geometrical puzzle on paper without retracing any of their lines and without lifting their pencil from the paper. Once again, some participants had been told before-hand that their personality characteristics made them likely to end up alone in life. That group gave up on the puzzle-tracing activity substantially sooner than anyone else in the study. In other words, anticipating social isolation—even years in the future—reduced their motivation to persevere with a complex cognitive task.

Ask Yourself

Do you ever lose focus when you feel lonely or disconnected?

The participants in these studies weren't mentally ill, nor did they suffer from disorders that would have limited their ability to think or concentrate, such as dementia or attention deficit hyper-activity disorder (ADHD). They were simply regular people who had been primed to think they would end up alone—and that was enough to hamper their cognitive abilities, at least for a time.

Disconnection Harms Social Wellness

Finally—and perhaps least surprisingly—people who feel lonely and affection deprived have problems relating socially to others. They are less likely to be married or in a significant romantic rela-tionship, for instance. And, among those who do have romantic partners, they report less satisfaction with their relationships if they don't receive as much affection as they wish. It's not a surprise, therefore, that a lack of affection is among the most common rea-sons why people split up. One study found that 79 percent of couples cited "losing a sense of closeness" and 67 percent cited "not feeling loved and appreciated by spouse" as reasons for their divorce. Indeed, these were the two most commonly cited out of a list of twenty-eight different reasons for ending their marriages. Moreover, *alienation of affection*—that is, leaving the marriage in order to pursue romantic involvement with someone else—has long been considered grounds for divorce.

To repeat an earlier point, the link between affection deprivation and divorce (or the demise of any significant relationship) probably operates in more than one direction:

1. On one hand, not getting enough love and affection from your partner could lead you to consider ending your relationship.
2. On the other hand, if your relationship is in distress and on the path to dissolution, your partner probably isn't giving you the affection you need.

Each condition—affection deprivation and relationship distress—can therefore contribute to the other. Consequently, the association between them is strong.

Socially disconnected people have other social deficits as well. For one, they're less generous and less willing to help others. Psychologists have found that when people feel excluded and alone, they become less cooperative, less generous with their time, less willing to donate money to a student fund, and less helpful after another person's mishap. They also become more aggressive toward others—for example, issuing more negative job evaluations of other people and blasting others with louder levels of obnoxious noise, even when the targets of their aggression have done nothing to provoke them. In short, people don't "play nice" when they feel excluded by others.

Our need to belong is extremely strong, so feeling alone and left out is a distressing state for most people. That's a huge part of the reason why bullying is so emotionally damaging for victims—being made to feel like you don't belong goes against our fundamental grain as human beings. Exclusion is so distressing, in fact, that even the *threat* of it can change people's behaviors dramatically. Organizations that enforce codes of morality and ethical behavior—such as churches or the military—often use the threat of exclusion effectively to modify the behaviors of errant members.

Marisa's Story

IT WAS MARISA'S YOUNGER BROTHER WHO INTRODUCED HER TO THE CHURCH SHE ATTENDED UNTIL RECENTLY. THE FIRST TIME SHE CAME TO A SERVICE, SHE WAS IMMEDIATELY SURROUNDED BY PEOPLE WHO MADE HER FEEL WELCOMED AND APPRECIATED. THEY TOLD HER SHE HAD FOUND HER HOME, AND THEY EAGERLY HELPED HER WITH ANYTHING SHE NEEDED, EVEN LENDING HER MONEY TO FIX THE AIR CONDITIONER IN HER CAR. MARISA QUICKLY GREW TO LOVE THE OTHERS IN HER CHURCH, AND SHE BELIEVED SINCERELY THAT THEY LOVED HER, TOO . . . UNTIL SHE STARTED QUESTIONING SOME OF THE CHURCH'S TEACHINGS. ONCE THAT HAPPENED, THE LOVE SHE HAD ENJOYED IN ABUNDANCE QUICKLY DRIED UP. SEVERAL OF HER FORMER "FRIENDS" EVEN STOPPED SPEAKING TO HER FOR A WHILE. IT WAS THEN THAT MARISA REALIZED THEIR AFFECTION HAD NEVER BEEN GENUINE IN THE FIRST PLACE, BUT HAD ALWAYS HAD AN UNDERLYING MOTIVE: TO MAKE HER BELIEVE AS THEY DID.

Many religious institutions, for instance, use social exclusion (in the form of excommunication, disfellowship, or shunning) to censure and punish those who don't accept the required doctrines or who behave in ways counter to their beliefs. I grew up in such a church, where errant members were summarily cut off from contact. Like Marisa, members who strayed were told in no uncertain terms that they were no longer welcome, and the rest of the congregation was threatened with excommunication themselves if they had contact with those who were excluded. When I was around the age of twelve, for example, I was told I could no longer speak to my aunt, uncle, or cousins because they had been cut off from the church, and in fact I didn't speak to any of them for years, out of fear of being excluded myself.

I don't defend this practice—in fact, I think it is extremely harmful—but I can't dispute its effectiveness at keeping a social group regulated. The mere threat of exclusion is often sufficient to keep people toeing the line, even if their adherence to expectations is motivated only by their fear of being kicked out of the club.

If we consider all of the research on pain, physical health problems, health-care habits, mental disorders, cognitive challenges, and social well-being in tandem, our conclusion is clear: Social disconnection is bad for us. The following table reminds us of the problems that research has shown to be associated with loneliness, social isolation, and/or affection deprivation. The bad news unfortunately doesn't end here, however. Not only do socially deprived people often suffer from a range of afflictions; many of them also cope with their disconnection in ways that do more harm than good. We'll explore some of these maladaptive coping strategies in the next chapter.

LONELINESS, SOCIAL ISOLATION, AND/OR AFFECTION DEPRIVATION ARE ASSOCIATED WITH . . .

MORE/HIGHER	LESS/LOWER
Physical pain	Quality sleep
Epstein-Barr virus activity	Natural killer cell activity
Secondary immune disorders	Exercise
Obesity, blood pressure, cholesterol	General mental well-being
Likelihood of smoking	Happiness
Calories consumed from fat	Ability to concentrate
Depression	Ability to persevere
Anxiety/mood disorders	Likelihood of a significant relationship
Alexithymia	Relationship satisfaction
Aggression toward others	Generosity with others

What Social Disconnection Doesn't Harm

My focus in this chapter has been on the high cost of social disconnection—that is, its many detriments in terms of physical, mental, cognitive, and relational health. It's important to point out, however, that affection deprivation, loneliness, and social exclusion don't impair every single aspect of a person's life. Socially disconnected people are no less intelligent, physically attractive, academically successful, or financially well off than their better-connected counterparts, for instance. They are no less socially skilled, and they're no more likely to have suffered traumatic events in their lives. As harmful as social disconnection can be, it's useful to remind ourselves that it doesn't invade every corner of a person's world.

Because disconnection is associated with problems in so many different realms, however, people try in various ways—many of them unsuccessful—to get more affection in their lives. And those who don't or can't get more affection often cope with their disconnection in ways that are ultimately self-destructive. We'll explore both in the next chapter.

Stop and Reflect

In this chapter, we have explored many of the physical and mental health problems that go along with feeling lonely, disconnected, and deprived of affection. Before proceeding to Chapter Six, consider your response to these queries:

- In your life, do you know anyone who feels lonely and isolated enough that he or she might contemplate suicide? Have you ever contemplated it yourself?
- Think of a time when you felt excluded by others. How did that make you feel physically, emotionally, and psychologically?
- Have you ever noticed that you take better care of yourself when you're happy with your relationships than when you aren't? If so, in what ways?

CHAPTER SIX

The Misguided Paths We Follow

Albert Einstein defined *insanity* as doing the same thing over and over again while expecting different results. When trying to solve a problem, though, it can be easy to get stuck in an unproductive pattern, trying the same approach time and again simply because we don't know what else to do.

That's the case for many people who experience affection hunger. When we feel deprived of something we need or want, our deprivation usually motivates us to get more of it. Hunger prompts us to find food, thirst motivates us to find water, and so forth—and once we get what we're after, we no longer feel as deprived. One of the reasons people stay in a state of affection deprivation, though, is that they get stuck making the same mistakes over time, trying and failing to attract the affection they want. Because they're unsuccessful at reducing their affection hunger, they often cope with their deprivation in unconstructive ways. This chapter examines both the common mistakes people make and the problematic coping strategies they often adopt.

Trying Unsuccessfully to Get More Affection

In my research on affection deprivation, one of the questions I sometimes ask people is what they have tried—unsuccessfully—to get more affection in their lives. In other words, what mistakes do people make when attempting to attract affection from others? If you feel hungry for affection yourself, this is a useful question to ponder for at least two reasons:

1. Perhaps you've tried similar strategies and wondered why they aren't as effective as you wish. I'll describe some of the shortcomings of these strategies in this section.
2. Learning from the mistakes of others can help you avoid making similar mistakes in your own relationships.

By no means are these the only mistakes a person can make when trying to attract more affection. Neither are these mistakes listed in any particular order. Consider them an informative snapshot of the struggles people describe when trying to address their affection hunger. My goal here is to identify and illustrate these mistakes—I'll offer constructive ways to attract more affection in the third section of this book.

Mistake: Demanding Instead of Inviting

Advice on how to better yourself—whether in the form of books, magazine articles, or Twitter teasers—has a way of inspiring a take-charge attitude. When you read about how to get better sex, conquer your social anxiety, win a promotion, or "get anyone to fall in love with you in just minutes," you find that the advice is often of this variety: *Figure out what you want and don't stop demanding it until you get it.* When we call this approach "being proactive," it sounds pretty positive—and perhaps it works for certain outcomes. It rarely works for affection, though.

Not getting the affection you want or need is frustrating, and that's especially true when the person holding out on you is your spouse or partner. We don't all come from affectionate families or have affectionate friends, but many of us believe that *we should at least* get affection in our romantic relationship. The frustration that ensues when we don't can lead us to react in some unconstructive ways, one of which is simply to demand more affection from someone else.

Kris, aged thirty-three, often feels this way in her relationship with her fiancé Brad. She explains that they are "in a constant struggle. I always crave more affection from him, and I expect it, given that I express it toward him. I think I don't receive as much as I want because I have a constant expectation that there should be a *certain level*." Of course, there's nothing inherently wrong with wanting more affection than you receive—many of us do—but Kris realizes that her expectations might be a bit unrealistic. What's more, she acknowledges that she sometimes tries to get more affection from Brad in a problematic way. As she explains, "I have tried vocalizing exactly what I need, but I tend to put too much attention on it, and that makes it awkward for my partner."

Kris's situation is not at all uncommon. She knows she wants a certain level of affection from Brad, and that it's more than he provides. Beyond the affection she *wants*, though, there is a level of affection she feels she *deserves*, given what she expresses to him. Affection normally carries a strong expectation of reciprocity—

when most of us say "I love you" to someone, we expect to hear it back. Kris perceives that she is giving Brad more affection than she receives in return, creating a sense of disparity in her mind.

To improve her situation, she has done exactly what many self-help books recommend: being upfront and straightforward about what she wants. For some people, hearing that message (*I want you to be more affectionate with me*) is a call to action that they are prepared to answer. Some of us may simply not realize we haven't been as affectionate as our partners want, and we appreciate finding that out, so we can pay more attention to our behavior. For others, though, the message that our partners want more affection brings stress. First, it draws attention to our shortcoming, by pointing out that we haven't been affectionate enough, making us feel neglectful or insensitive. Second, it can pressure us into behaving in ways that may not feel natural.

Did You Know?

Some people curtail their affection specifically to avoid making others feel obligated to reciprocate.

I don't know Kris and Brad personally, so beyond what they tell me, I can't presume to know how they feel. With that caveat, let me use them to illustrate a hypothetical situation, one that many women and men can probably relate to. Kris and Brad love each other. Precisely *because* she loves Brad, Kris expresses affection to him and craves the same from him. Presumably, Brad communicates his love to some degree, but not with the frequency or intensity that Kris wants and feels she deserves. So, she tells Brad she wants more. She might indicate, for instance, that she wants him to say "I love you" more often. Even though she knows that Brad loves her, his infrequency in saying so makes her *feel* unloved. In her mind, if Brad genuinely loves her, he should have no problem saying it . . . and a bit more often, thank you very much.

Brad perceives that he says "I love you" when he truly feels it. He acknowledges that Kris wants more affection from him, but in his mind, asking him to say he loves her more often is not the answer. If he says it because he feels it, that's fine—but if he says it because she's asked him to, it feels fraudulent. Kris might counter that point by noting that if Brad really loves her, he shouldn't have a problem saying so. To Brad, his feelings for Kris aren't the issue—he loves her dearly. Saying "I love you" doesn't seem genuine to him, though, when he feels *expected* to say it.

Although she wouldn't describe it in this way, Kris makes the mistake of *demanding* expressions of affection from Brad. Even if she wouldn't use that term, she would be the first to acknowledge that her approach is often unsuccessful.

Mistake: Ignoring the Forms of Affection You Already Receive

In my research over the last two decades, one of the most compelling findings has been the level of diversity that exists in how people communicate affection to each other. We use a broad range of behaviors to convey love and appreciation for the people in our lives. Some affection displays are overt and obvious, such as kissing, holding hands, hugging, and saying "I love you." Many other expressions are less overt and obvious in their meaning, but to receivers who acknowledge them, they are nonetheless *meaningful*.

For example, when I've asked people how they show affection to their spouses, I almost always get different answers from women and men. Women take the overt, demonstrative route by verbalizing their feelings directly and using nonverbal behaviors such as kissing, tender touching, and handholding. Men take a more pragmatic approach, often preferring to show their love in more instrumental ways, such as by taking care of important household tasks. It seems that men, on average, like to convey their affection by *doing things*—washing the car without asking, picking up groceries unexpectedly, watching the kids so their wives can have a girls' night out. Many men seem to believe, at least implicitly, that *saying* you love someone is less valuable than *showing* it through your actions.

Certainly, some men focus on instrumental displays because they're uncomfortable communicating affection in more overt ways. Quite often, though, men's instrumental affection displays are every bit as meaningful in their minds as more overt expressions. Alex, thirty-seven years old, says, "I show my wife I love her by doing things I know she'll appreciate, like having the house cleaned up and a nice dinner on the table when she's had a long day at school." Alex believes that his wife, Katy, not only appreciates these gestures but *interprets them as expressions of his affection for her*, which is how he intends them.

In many relationships, though, a common mistake—especially for women—is not to recognize or value the affectionate expressions they already receive. DeAnn, aged fifty-seven, explains that she often overlooked the affectionate gestures of her late husband, Shane, who lost his life to lung cancer in his mid-fifties. "I was always on his case," she says. "I think a woman needs a certain level of affection from her husband to feel secure, at least I did . . . but Shane was never the expressive type, you know? He wasn't raised to be emotional." As a result, DeAnn says, she frequently felt like Shane didn't love her as much as she loved him, because he didn't convey his affection in the same ways she did.

Shane's death at an early age was understandably devastating for DeAnn, and it caused her to do some serious soul-searching about many aspects of her life, including her marriage. It was during that time that she realized how many things Shane did to show his affection for her—things she never recognized as expressions of love. She recalls one incident, in particular, when their daughter (who lived in another state) suffered a devastating miscarriage. "I'm sure he [Shane] was suffering too, but he saw how sad I was and he put his own feelings aside to help me. He called my manager and told her I needed to be with my daughter, and they worked it out for me to be gone. And he got me a ticket and drove me to the train, and all I could think about was being with my daughter. Shane took care of everything for us to be together, not even worrying about his own grief from losing a grandchild."

Given her distressed state, DeAnn didn't recognize it at the time, but this was one example of Shane expressing affection through his actions. As she reflected on their marriage, she recalled many similar instances, and discovered that she had never realized just how affectionate Shane was.

None of this is to say that a woman can't prefer more overt forms of affection—more kisses, more "I love you"s—from her husband or partner. It's a mistake, however, to overlook forms of affection they are already receiving, for at least two reasons. First, doing so makes their affection deprivation seem worse than it is.

Recall the point I have made several times in this book: Deprivation is the difference between what you want and what you get. It's important to be honest about what you want, but it is also important to be accurate about what you are already getting, because failing to do either can make you feel more deprived than necessary.

Victor's Story

VICTOR AND HIS WIFE SHERREE HAVE BEEN MARRIED FOR FOURTEEN YEARS, AND FOR THE LAST THREE YEARS SHERREE HAS COMPLAINED TO HER SISTERS AND FRIENDS ABOUT HOW SHE WANTS VICTOR TO BE MORE LOVING. VICTOR FINDS THIS EXASPERATING. RIGHT AFTER THEY GOT MARRIED, HE QUIT HIS JOB AND MOVED TO CONNECTICUT WITH HER SO SHE COULD GO TO LAW SCHOOL. IN THE WINTER, HE ALWAYS MAKES SURE HER CAR HAS A FULL TANK OF GAS AND IS STOCKED WITH EMERGENCY SUPPLIES IN CASE SHE GETS STUCK SOMEWHERE. HE LOOKS AFTER EVERYTHING AROUND THEIR HOUSE, PAYS THE BILLS, AND ALWAYS MAKES SURE THE YARD LOOKS NICE. IN HIS MIND, THERE'S ONLY ONE REASON HE DOES ALL THESE THINGS: IT'S BECAUSE HE LOVES SHERREE SO MUCH. WHEN HE HEARS ABOUT HER COMPLAINTS, HE WONDERS TO HIMSELF, "HOW MUCH MORE LOVING DOES SHE NEED ME TO BE?"

Second, when men's instrumental ways of expressing affection go unacknowledged, men understandably feel that their affection itself is unvalued. This is how Victor feels. If I communicate love to my spouse by washing her car every week, that to me is a genuine expression of my feelings. If she doesn't take it as such, though, then it's easy for me to feel that my affection for her is unappreciated—just as she would feel if she wrote me a loving card that I didn't acknowledge.

I have framed my discussion of this mistake in the language of sex differences because, *on average*, it is men who express affection through instrumental behaviors and women who sometimes don't recognize those expressions. Like any generalization, of course, that statement has exceptions: Instrumental expressions of affection can be enacted—and overlooked—by either sex. Whatever the specifics, the heart of the problem is a lack of awareness that there are many ways, some more "covert" than others, to communicate feelings of love.

Mistake: Sexualizing Affection

In romantic relationships—whether established or budding—people often show their affection for each other sexually. Sex can certainly be casual or recreational, but it can also be an intense and intimate way of expressing romantic love.

Humans value sex for many reasons, not the least of which is simply that it feels good. It's therefore not surprising that people are willing to barter to get it. In the case of prostitution, it's a direct exchange of money for sex . . . but that isn't the only example. People trade for sexual access, whether with economic goods (providing a paycheck, offering gifts), the expenditure of time and attention, a promise of future commitment, a relinquishment of other sexual opportunities, or emotional submission (in the form of apologizing, groveling, or begging). Indeed, sex is exchanged for any or all of these resources, even in marriages and other established relationships.

Did You Know?

Sexual orgasm causes a substantial increase in oxytocin for both women and men, which researchers believe contributes to feelings of intimacy between sexual partners.

When it comes to exchanging something of value for sex, there's little point in pretending that women and men are on equal ground. A principle called *minimal parental investment* explains that in any species (including humans), the sex who invests more resources to produce offspring is the one that is choosiest when it comes to granting sexual access. Usually, that's the female. To produce a child, for instance, a woman invests one of her finite number of eggs, becomes impregnated, carries the pregnancy to term over nine months, and then endangers her own health and survival by delivering the baby. In this process, she has paid dearly in terms of the stress and strain on her body and in terms of her lost social, economic, and professional opportunities. In sharp contrast, the man's investment represents a single sperm cell (of which he can produce virtually an unlimited supply), the time and energy it takes to impregnate the woman, and whatever resources he spent in pursuit of that mating opportunity.

These are the *minimum* investments required to produce a child, so I don't describe this to trivialize the fact that most people—men *and* women—invest much, much more in their children. I bring it up because the stark difference in the *required* investment means that pregnancy is substantially costlier for women than for men, and that's why women are choosier when it comes to sex. It's not an accident that most prostitutes are women and most customers are men. It's also not a fluke that, even in close relationships, it's the woman who decides when—or if—sex occurs. It's evolution-ary . . . and it's the same across species.

Did You Know?

In the potbellied seahorse (*Hippocampus abdominalis*), it's the male who carries and gives birth to offspring. In that species, therefore, males are sexually choosier than females.

Women thus have the opportunity to request (or demand) what they want in exchange for granting sexual access. Some women ask for jewelry, some for protection, and some for a mar-riage proposal. Women who feel affection deprived, however, may use sex as a means of getting affection. Rose, aged fifty-nine, rec-ognized that pattern in herself when she told me, "Unfortunately the way I sought affection was through intimate relations with many men. My relationships seemed to go right to the bedroom and never developed into anything deep or meaningful. It left me feeling empty and hollow inside."

Brianna, forty-four years of age, was similar. When I asked her to describe her unsuccessful attempts to attract affection, she replied, "I sexualized myself quite a bit. Although I was safe, I was very promiscuous." Like Rose, Brianna goes on to describe using sex as a way to get affection, which she now regrets. When I asked her what advice she would have for people who feel affec-tion deprived, she said, "Don't use your body, or sexualize your-self, because after you have, you likely feel worse. I know I did. Because afterward, they're gone, and the best parts of cuddling or eating together in bed are nowhere, because there is no real connection." Although Rose and Brianna have used sex to attract affection outside of established relationships, forty-six-year-old Liz admitted doing the same in her marriage: "I have used sex to get more affection from my husband. It worked in the moment—but in the long term, maybe not."

Liz's observation is important: Offering sex in exchange for expressions of affection is sometimes an effective *short-term* strategy. We have all known men who will say anything, including "I love you," if the opportunity for sex presents itself. When such a man is paired with a woman who wants to hear that phrase, he recognizes that saying it will get him what he wants, and she realizes that allowing him sex will get her what she wants. This kind of exchange, although common, is somewhat hollow, because although he is getting a genuine sexual encounter, she is getting only the *appearance* of affection. He knows that saying "I love you" is easy—and perhaps especially so when he doesn't mean it. It is, therefore, a small price to pay for the sexual opportunity. Although she gets what she wants in the short term—to be told that she is loved—her gain is temporal and fleeting. Thus, it's not effective as a long-term solution to her affection needs.

Mistake: Expecting a Specific Person to Meet Your Affection Needs

We don't *learn* to need affection, the way we learn to walk, speak, or ride a bike. As I explained in the first section of the book, our need for affection is with us at birth—and in the early days of our lives, we look to our parents to meet those needs. The care and affection an infant requires *can* come from anyone, but in most cases, it's primarily the infant's mother who provides. And, so long as its needs are met, an infant isn't bothered by getting all of his or her affection from one person.

As we grow, though, many of us make the mistake of continuing to expect one specific person—whether a parent, a romantic partner, a friend—to provide us with the affection we need. Instead of cultivating a range of relationships that can fulfill our desires for love and affection, we pin all our hopes—and pile all the pressure—onto one individual.

Anna, fifty-two years of age, recalls doing this with her mom. "My mother was a very distant person," Anna explains. "She avoided looking at me, wasn't interested in having a conversation with me, unless it was for her to unload about her problems, and was extremely critical." According to Anna, her mother's demeanor kept her from expressing the affection that Anna craved. "She did not touch me, nor did she touch my children. When I moved overseas, I would come home for visits. My mother-in-law would give me a hug and kiss and my mother would just stand there and say hello. I wanted to hug her but felt it would not be welcome." Anna recalls an epiphany that occurred with her mother's death. "When she died I spent thirty minutes just stroking her hair. It was the first time in my life I had been allowed to touch her and I had a real need to do it. When I did not get the affection I needed from my mother I felt rejected, unloved, sad, [and] it was hard to cope with bad things that happened. I felt very isolated and alone."

Anna's story illustrates a common conundrum: We all need affection, but not everyone is capable of providing it. Many of us want or expect a specific person in our lives, such as a spouse or parent, to meet our affection needs . . . and it certainly isn't a mistake to try what we can to attract more affection from that person. We err, though, when we fail to recognize that some people are incapable of meeting our affection needs, no matter what we try.

It's understandable that you might find that statement hard to accept. With a spouse or romantic partner in particular, many of us feel we have *the right* to expect that person to meet our affection needs. After all, isn't that sort of implied in the notion of a romantic relationship?

That right may indeed be implied when we establish a close relationship, but this expectation isn't always realistic. Some people, such as Anna's mother, find it hard to express virtually any form of affection to others. There are many possible reasons why that's the case, and I'm not passing judgment on those who find affection difficult. Continuing to expect such people to provide you with affection, however, is like expecting a blind person to see and then feeling hurt when he cannot.

To her great credit, Anna has found many other people in her life who are willing *and capable* of giving her the affection she desires, so she may not feel a sense of affection hunger overall. It is certainly very sad when someone we love and care for is unable to express the affection we crave from him or her, but that is sometimes the reality, and it is a mistake not to accept it when it is. In many such cases, we can maintain a relationship with the person—as Anna did with her mother—without continuing to expect affection that the person can't deliver.

On occasion, however, our best option may actually be ending the relationship. Understandably, that's often a difficult decision to make, because it means giving up—not only on our *hopes* for the relationship, but on the relationship itself. In a marriage, for example, people who feel they require affection from their spouses to be happy, but who are married to spouses incapable of meeting that need, may find their happiness permanently restrained unless they are willing to make a change. They can choose either to change their needs and expectations regarding the marriage, making the lack of spousal affection less distressing, or they can end the marriage and seek a more affectionate spouse. Not everyone is willing to do that, and not everyone should . . . but if your need for spousal affection is too great to change and your spouse is unable to meet it, then it is an option that deserves consideration.

Ask Yourself

Besides the four mistakes described here, what other mistakes have you made (if any) when trying to attract more affection? Why were these strategies unsuccessful?

These four mistakes—demanding affection instead of inviting it; ignoring forms of affection you already receive; sexualizing affection; and expecting a specific person to meet your needs— are certainly not the only mistakes people make. Desperation can drive people to make the same poor decisions over and over again, trying failed strategies to get more affection in their lives. The mistakes involved in affection hunger don't end there, however. Unfortunately, many people cope with their lack of social connection in ways that are not only unhelpful, but ultimately harmful. Let's take a closer look at some of the poorest coping strategies, many of which—sadly—are common among the lonely and disconnected.

Coping with Disconnection

Affection is such a strong need that people who feel socially disconnected have to cope with their deprivation in some way:

- Some manage by reading romance novels or watching romantic movies and living vicariously through other people's intimacy.
- Others try to simulate interpersonal connection by immersing themselves in crowds, such as at a shopping mall or church service.
- Still others attempt to embrace their aloneness by practicing meditation or communing with nature.

These kinds of coping mechanisms—even if they don't actually increase affection—can at least benefit people in other ways. At the very least, their effects are benign, not helping people but not hurting them, either.

Unfortunately, not everyone manages in constructive ways. The need for affection is great, so being affection deprived is a difficult state, one that can motivate some less-than-helpful coping strategies. As we review some of the most common unconstructive methods of coping with disconnection, bear in mind that they aren't always mutually exclusive. People who adopt one of these behaviors often adopt others as well, which only compounds their harmful effects.

Risky Sexual Behavior

In the context of a close, satisfying relationship, sex is an important way to express and reinforce feelings of affection. Both the emotional intimacy of sex and its pleasurable physical sensations can do much to make a person feel accepted, appreciated, and loved. When people feel alone and disconnected, therefore, sexual contact with another person has the potential to alleviate those feelings, at least temporarily. Consider the stereotypical image of the lonely single man who deals with his loneliness by soliciting prostitutes. Although sex for money rarely involves any kind of emotional intimacy, the physical intimacy of the act can generate at least a temporal feeling of acceptance, connection, and even love.

It shouldn't be surprising, therefore, that some people cope with feelings of loneliness and social deprivation by engaging in risky sexual behaviors. That includes not only sex with prostitutes and escorts but also "hookups," those casual sexual encounters (often between strangers) that carry no expectations for commitment. Although these types of interactions can present both legal and financial risks, I highlight casual sex here primarily for its health risks. Specifically, both paid and unpaid sexual encounters frequently involve partners whose sexual history is unknown, whose previous partners are many, and whose observance of safe sexual practices may be less than diligent.

Despite the substantial risks, casual sexual hookups are common, widespread, and easier than ever to arrange. Multiple websites and apps—such as Tinder and Grindr—allow people to identify others in the same market. Many of these even pinpoint users' locations, so you can see who's available, interested, and close by. To be sure, people have motives beyond loneliness to engage in casual sex . . . nonetheless, social disconnection is a key factor. One study of young adults, for instance, found that higher levels of loneliness corresponded to more frequent sexual hookups. This is notable because engaging in casual sex—even if to soothe feelings of loneliness—elevates people's risk of contracting HIV and other sexually transmitted diseases (which, as we discussed in the previous chapter, is one possible reason why affection hunger is linked to secondary immune disorders such as AIDS).

Not to perpetuate a stereotype, but research shows that using casual sex as a coping strategy for loneliness is particularly common for men who have sex with men (whether they identify as homosexual or bisexual). Researchers in one study interviewed young men (ages eighteen to twenty-nine) about their sexual behaviors with other men. In their stories, the researchers found a cyclical pattern: When the men felt lonely, they "treated" their loneliness by having casual sex, which then made them worry about the possibility of contracting HIV, leading them to think negatively about themselves and eventually to feel lonely all over again. Although hookups were a common strategy for coping with loneliness, therefore, they were only temporarily effective. Sexual interaction provides a short-term connection with someone else, but it does not lessen feelings of loneliness in the long run.

Drug Use

One reason why sex—whether casual or not—temporarily improves feelings of loneliness is that, for a short while, it floods the brain with feel-good hormones such as oxytocin and dopamine. These chemicals make your body feel like a wonderland:

They reduce pain, promote calm, increase warmth, and generally impart sensations of pleasure. Of course, these effects last only as long as the hormone levels are elevated; once they return to their normal levels, the pleasurable sensations dissipate, leaving lonely people longing for another sexual encounter.

Another activity that increases pleasure-enhancing chemicals in the body is drug use. Many addictive substances—from caffeine and nicotine to heroin and cocaine—are addictive precisely because they elevate levels of dopamine. It's the dopamine boost that makes the drug feel good.

Bill's Story

BILL STARTED SMOKING IN HIGH SCHOOL AS A WAY TO FIT IN: ALL OF HIS FRIENDS SMOKED, AND HE LIKED FEELING INCLUDED. AFTER HIS WIFE LEFT HIM AND A DOWNTURN IN THE REAL ESTATE MARKET COST HIM HIS JOB AS A ROOFER, HE FELT VERY ALONE AND STARTED SHOOTING HEROIN TO MAKE HIMSELF FEEL BETTER. IT WORKED, AT LEAST FOR A WHILE. NOT ONLY DID THE DRUG MAKE HIM EUPHORIC, BUT HE WAS SHOOTING UP WITH SOME OF THE GUYS HE USED TO WORK WITH, WHICH MADE HIM FEEL LESS ALONE.

When framed in this way, it's easy to understand why drug use is a common coping strategy for people who are unhappy with their lives. At least on a temporary basis, the dopamine boost that comes from downing espresso or smoking crack gives users an elevated sense of pleasure, relief, and escape from what ails them. It's not surprising, therefore, to find that people like Bill use drugs as a way to cope with the pain of social disconnection. According to research, loneliness and exclusion don't correspond to caffeine use. They do, however, predict people's tendencies to use more harmful illicit drugs, including marijuana, cocaine, heroin, and crystal meth.

As coping strategies go, this one is fraught with many obvious dangers. In exchange for temporary bouts of relief from loneliness or affection hunger, drug users expose themselves to a range of serious problems:

1. There are the legal risks of buying and using substances that are unlawful in most jurisdictions.
2. There are the financial problems that accompany spending significant amounts of money to support a drug habit.
3. Finally, there's a variety of substantial health risks, which include tissue damage, respiratory distress, exposure to hepatitis or HIV, and premature death from overdose.

The fact that loneliness encourages people to take such risks by using drugs speaks volumes about how painful a situation social disconnection can be.

Ask Yourself

Even if you've never used illicit drugs, do you ever drink alcohol or smoke cigarettes specifically to soothe feelings of loneliness?

Gambling

Using drugs isn't the only way to get a dopamine hit. Some people experience the same rush when they gamble.

Many gamblers, if not most, partake only occasionally. They gamble for entertainment or to pass the time, never betting more than they can afford to lose. We might think of them as "controlled gamblers," similar to people who drink but don't have a drinking problem. Gambling becomes a problem, though, when it starts to interfere with work, damage relationships, or strain financial resources. It turns into an obsession when people can't stop thinking about it, and it becomes a compulsion when they continue gambling regardless of the consequences. Whether they're broke or flush, depressed or happy, compulsive gamblers can't seem to break the habit. Although we might say that such a person is "addicted to gambling," the American Psychiatric Association classifies *pathological gambling* as an impulse-control disorder—an inability to resist even harmful temptations or urges—rather than an addiction. Whether pathological or just problematic, uncontrolled gambling can destroy marriages, careers, and lives.

As with casual sex and drug use, gambling behavior has a relationship with feelings of social disconnection. Several studies have found that loneliness and isolation are substantially more common for people who gamble than for people who don't. In one study of adolescents, for example, 6 percent cited loneliness as one of their reasons for gambling. Even *among* gamblers, research shows that social disconnection is much more pronounced for those whose gambling is problematic or pathological, rather than controlled.

There are a few reasons why lonely or affection-deprived people might use gambling as a coping strategy:

1. The thrill of gambling may provide a pleasurable dopamine rush, similar to what some people experience when they use drugs.

2. Many gambling activities take place in social environments, such as casinos, where a socially disconnected person has the opportunity to meet and interact with other people, many of whom are in a good mood and having fun. (Not all gambling occurs in such environments, of course; many people gamble online while physically alone.)

3. Gambling simply provides people with something entertaining to occupy their time and to distract them from thinking about their social isolation.

To varying degrees, gambling might be a coping strategy for all three of these reasons. And, if done responsibly, it may well be an *effective* strategy for dealing with the pains of social isolation, because it provides an opportunity for entertainment and social contact. It's when people start neglecting their jobs, their families, and their finances in order to support a compulsive gambling habit that this coping mechanism becomes harmful.

Loneliness appears to be a stronger predictor of risky gambling by women than by men. In one study, 829 young adults who said they gambled at least occasionally were assessed in terms of their gambling-related problems, and they were ultimately divided into two groups: controlled gamblers and at-risk gamblers. Men were more likely than women to be at-risk gamblers, but loneliness predicted at-risk gambling for women only. Other research has found the same. Although men are more likely to be problematic gamblers, therefore, they aren't as likely as women to gamble *because of loneliness*. It may be that women who feel socially disconnected see gambling as a safe alternative to casual sex or drug use, and use it as a coping strategy for that reason.

Disordered Eating

A fourth coping mechanism related to feelings of affection deprivation is disordered eating. Eating disorders are classified as mental illnesses by the American Psychiatric Association, and they come in three basic forms:

1. *Anorexia nervosa,* characterized by severe calorie restriction and an obsession with thinness.
2. *Bulimia nervosa,* typified by repeatedly eating large quantities of food and then purging through vomiting or laxative abuse.
3. *Binge eating disorder,* characterized by excessive eating without subsequent purging.

All three disorders are dangerous for physical health, increasing the odds of heart problems, ulcers, kidney failure, and premature death.

Doing drugs, having sex, and gambling each alter the body's chemical state in ways that temporarily bring pleasure and reduce pain; thus, it's easy to understand why they are used as strategies for coping with social disconnection. Why would affection deprivation or loneliness be related to disordered eating, though? One answer is that an eating disorder—especially anorexia—can take on a life of its own and be seen almost as a partner. As physician

Martha Peaslee Levine explains, "The illness is viewed as a friend who is always there." Levine quotes a participant from one eating disorder study who described her anorexia as "a marriage or relationship. . . . it is always there for me, stopping me feeling alone." In this way, eating disorders function as companions, giving socially disconnected sufferers something they can rely on and pay attention to instead of their loneliness.

Bulimia and binge eating disorder may also be coping strategies because eating food has soothing effects. As psychologists John Cacioppo and William Patrick point out in their book, *Loneliness: Human Nature and the Need for Social Connection*, the lining of the human digestive system has the same developmental roots as the skin, so ingesting food feels like a kind of internal massage. "Eating is a way of self-soothing that carries costs when we take it to excess," they note, "but that does not make it any less soothing in the moment."

Feelings of social isolation are a risk factor for the development of all three eating disorders, but especially binge eating disorder. Feeling alone, in other words, makes people want to eat more than they should—perhaps, as mentioned, because the sensations that go along with ingesting food are physically and emotionally comforting, especially for people who lack such comforting in their interpersonal relationships.

It's not necessary to have been formally diagnosed with anorexia, bulimia, or binge eating, however, to have disordered eating habits. Research shows that loneliness affects the amount of food we eat, even if we don't technically have an eating disorder. According to one study, the effects of loneliness on food consumption depend on whether people are already restricting their intake through dieting. Those on a diet eat more food than normal when they feel lonely, whereas those who aren't dieting eat less than usual. Either pattern can lead to problems if it represents a departure from healthy eating behaviors.

Did You Know?

Feelings of social isolation also make it more difficult for people to recover from eating disorders, increasing their odds of relapse.

Suicide

In the most desperate of cases, people cope with their loneliness by taking their own lives—the very antithesis of a healthy coping mechanism. Some are like Seth Walsh, whom we met in Chapter Five: teased, bullied, and rejected by their own peers. Others simply feel alone, forgotten, and inconsequential in the world. Regardless of their circumstances, those who feel socially disconnected can reach a point when no other methods of coping have worked and suicide seems like the only remaining option.

For obvious reasons, it's impossible to collect data about loneliness or affection hunger from people who have committed suicide. As an alternative, researchers examine two closely related phenomena: *suicidal ideation*, which is the tendency to contemplate killing oneself, and *parasuicide*, which is an unsuccessful suicide attempt. Both are strongly associated with loneliness. In one study involving nearly 20,000 people aged fifteen or older, researchers investigated whether suicidal ideation and parasuicide were related to the experiences of living alone, having no close friends, and frequently feeling lonely. All three experiences were associated with the suicide outcomes. In other words, both *thoughts of suicide* and *attempts at suicide* were more common for people who lived alone (vs. living with others), had no friends (vs. had close friends), and felt lonely (vs. not feeling lonely).

Importantly, the feeling of loneliness was the most powerful factor out of the three. That is, even if participants had close friends and/or lived with other people, they were still at increased risk of suicidal ideation and parasuicide if they felt lonely. In fact, *lonely people were twelve-and-a-half times as likely as non-lonely people to attempt suicide.*

Perhaps more than any other research findings I've discussed in this book, these observations should give us pause. It's one thing if feeling socially deprived makes you risk your well-being by lighting up a joint, betting your wages at the racetrack, or hooking up with a stranger. It's quite a different story when it motivates you to end your life. This point, I think, helps us appreciate the true gravity of affection deprivation, loneliness, and social isolation. Some see the experience of disconnection as a nuisance, or as a source of dissatisfaction with life. For some people, though, it is a reason to stop living . . . and those who contemplate or attempt suicide are more likely to succeed in eventually ending their lives.

A Better Way

So far in this book, we have seen that humans need close, affectionate relationships in their lives in order to be happy and healthy. When we meet our relational needs, we thrive—and when we don't, we falter. Some of us try unsuccessfully to get more affection in our lives, and some of us cope with our lack of social connection in unhealthy and self-destructive ways.

Maybe you're one of those people who has wanted more intimacy, closeness, and affection than you get and has tried without success to change your situation. Even if you have coped with your lack of affection in healthy ways—never resorting, say, to compulsive gambling or random sexual hookups—perhaps you still have a sense of despair, an emptiness that makes you feel you'll never be loved the way you want.

The good news is you can take steps, beginning today, to attract more of the affection you hunger for. In the third and final section of the book, you'll find six specific recommendations that can start you on your path to a more affectionate life.

Stop and Reflect

We have seen in this chapter that people often try misguided paths to attract more affection, and cope with feelings of disconnection in some counterproductive ways. Consider these questions before you proceed to Chapter Seven:

- When, if ever, have you expected a specific person to meet all or most of your affection needs? Was that person successful at doing so?
- Even if you have never engaged in casual sex, have you ever consented to sex in order to feel less alone? Was that strategy successful?
- Besides the problems described in this chapter, in what ways have you coped with loneliness that have been counterproductive? What strategies would have been more productive?

PART THREE

Six Strategies to Overcome Loneliness

Thus far we have come to understand the important role that affection plays in our lives, explored the benefits of giving and receiving affection, considered the reasons why some people feel deprived of adequate affection, and investigated some of the many pitfalls that accompany a lack of close personal connections. The final part of the book is dedicated to remedies for loneliness and affection hunger. Each chapter in this part describes one strategy for inviting more affection into your life. Chapter Seven encourages you to change your understanding in order to remove any barriers that may be inhibiting your own affection with others. Chapter Eight suggests inviting affection instead of demanding it, and modeling the specific forms of affection you seek. In Chapter Nine, you're invited to recognize diversity in affection displays in order to acknowledge affection you may already be receiving but are unaware of. Chapter Ten suggests nurturing a wider variety of relationships, and Chapter Eleven reminds you to be aware of toxic forms of affection, those that carry unwanted obligations. Finally, we learn in Chapter Twelve to keep our expectations for affection both optimistic and realistic. As you read through these strategies, bear in mind that this is not a step-by-step program—some of the tactics may be more relevant for your circumstances than others. Approach these strategies with an open mind, and consider how each of them might apply in your own life.

CHAPTER SEVEN

Strategy #1: Be Open to Receiving Affection

One way we encourage more affection from others is to become more affectionate with them. Affectionate communication is a highly reciprocal behavior, meaning that people who receive affectionate expressions feel a strong sense of duty to respond in kind. When someone says "I love you," it's pretty difficult not to say the same back. Thus, if we want more affection from our loved ones, our simplest and most direct strategy is to give more to them.

That's often easier said than done, though. Many people are reluctant to express affection to others because of their own fears. *What if she doesn't feel the same way? What if he misinterprets what I'm saying?* These and other fears can lead people to suppress their own affectionate behavior, according to my research. For many people, that creates a real bind: They want others to be more affectionate with them, but at the same time, they keep others at arms' length because they fear being affectionate themselves. Thus, even though they want more affection, they're actually not open to it.

To invite more affection in your life, it's useful to consider whether your own affectionate behavior with other people is being stymied by fear. If it is, then a technique called *cognitive reframing* can help you change your understanding of the risks of affection so that your worries don't hold you back. The process starts with identifying your fears. It then involves reframing your concerns, and finally, operating from your new reality.

First, Identify Your Fears

Maintaining relationships may seem like the easiest and most natural thing in the world . . . and for some folks, it is. For many of us, though, expressing feelings of friendship, love, and appreciation makes us feel uncomfortable, so much so that we don't communicate our affection for others even when we feel it. Perhaps you know someone who is uncomfortable showing affection, or perhaps you are that person. In either case, identifying and understanding the fears that block affection is a critical first step toward combatting them. To do so, it's instructive to think about why we experience fear at all.

Know the Purpose of Fear

Fear has a pretty bad rep. As a society, we often associate *being afraid* with *being weak*, and we extol the virtues of bravery while claiming we have nothing to fear but fear itself. This paints such a negative picture of fear that many people are understandably reluctant to admit feeling it. In North American cultures, that's probably especially true for men, given that confidence, boldness, and heroism are all part of what we consider masculine. To some extent, men who are afraid aren't *real men*.

The problem with that understanding is that fear is an extraordinarily useful emotion. It represents our response to anything we believe poses a threat to our well-being. Some threats are physical, such as facing a serious illness, being robbed at gunpoint, or parachuting out of an airplane. Other threats are social, such as giving a speech, being embarrassed at a party, or getting a negative evaluation at work. Still other threats are economic, such as losing your retirement savings to a financial scam, or existential, such as facing eternal damnation for breaking a religious commandment.

Not everyone fears the same things, of course. For some, the prospect of giving a speech in front of an audience is terrifying, but after twenty-plus years of teaching, I'm quite comfortable with it. By the same token, I would be horrified to jump out of a plane, whereas it's a thrill for experienced skydivers. No matter the specifics, we feel fear when we perceive—accurately or inaccurately—that some aspect of our well-being is endangered. In most cases, fear encourages us to engage in fight or flight, wherein we try either to neutralize the threat (such as pursuing aggressive treatment for an illness or disagreeing with our negative work evaluation) or to get away from it (such as leaving a party after being embarrassed or suspending belief in the religious commandment we've broken).

As discomforting as fear can be, it's essential for our survival because it motivates us to respond to danger. It's good to be afraid of things that can hurt us, because our fear equips us to manage those threats properly and to avoid them whenever possible. If we weren't afraid of heights, for instance, we'd have no reason to be careful when using a ladder or crossing a suspension bridge, and harmful accidents would be more common. Fear alerts us to threat and it motivates us to protect ourselves as much as we can.

Explore Why You're Holding Back Your Affection

Expressing affection may seem like a strange behavior to list alongside jumping out of an airplane, experiencing armed robbery, or losing your life savings. The latter items all represent real threats to your physical or financial well-being, whereas it's easy to wonder why the same might be true of affection.

The truth is that *expressing affection can threaten our psychological and emotional well-being* in multiple ways. To appreciate how, let's look at the experiences of three individuals who suppress their affectionate behavior with loved ones out of fear:

- **Brady** (twenty-nine years old) has been dating his girlfriend Sophia for slightly more than a year. He knows he loves her, but communicating affection makes him uncomfortable. He is especially reluctant to say "I love you," which is what Sophia longs to hear. The problem is that expressing his affection makes Brady feel vulnerable, and he doesn't like feeling that way. He worries that if he "puts himself out there" by revealing his love directly, he opens himself up to possible rejection. Even as he wishes others were more affectionate with him, then, he curtails his own affection because of the vulnerability it creates.

- **Amanda** (forty-four years old) has a tendency to "come on too strong" with people she likes. In the past, when meeting a new friend or romantic partner, she has quickly smothered that person with affection. As a result, many promising relationships have fizzled because the person saw her as too "clingy" or emotionally needy. Amanda now recognizes how this tendency has hurt her in the past. To prevent the same mistakes, however, she has become overly cautious, almost to the point of being stingy with her affection. Although she craves affection from others, her fear of scaring off new friends or partners causes her to express it only sparingly.

- **Jack** (fifty-one years old) is what we might call "commitment phobic." For most of his adult life, he hasn't felt a strong need for close relationships, preferring instead to be independent and alone. When a new relationship does start to develop, he's afraid of being too affectionate because he doesn't want to commit himself to the other person too early or too strongly. He enjoys feeling loved by others, but he avoids expressing those feelings because he fears the commitment and obligation they imply.

Brady, Amanda, and Jack all enjoy receiving affection, but for various reasons, they are fearful about expressing it to others. Brady is afraid of vulnerability and rejection, Amanda worries about scaring people off, and Jack fears committing himself too deeply to someone else.

Attachment security is a person's ability to trust and count on the significant people in his or her life. We all find some folks more trustworthy and dependable than others, but the idea behind attachment security is that each of us has a particular *attachment style* that reflects our general approach to personal relationships. According to psychologist Kim Bartholomew, adults develop one of four attachment styles, and people who have the *secure style* are generally comfortable getting close to others and letting others get close to them.

Bartholomew explains that there are three types of insecure attachment:

1. Brady has what's called the *fearful style*, because he worries that he'll get rejected or hurt if he allows himself to be too close to others.

2. Amanda is an example of the *preoccupied style*, which means she wants more intimacy than she feels she gets, so she has overcompensated by suffocating people with attention and love until she scares them away.

3. Finally, Jack represents the *dismissive style*, in that he relies mostly on himself and shies away from commitment.

Many years of research have shown that people's attachment styles influence how they form and maintain relationships with others, including their level of comfort with affectionate expressions.

All of Brady, Amanda, and Jack's fears are reasonable—and on some level, they may even be useful at helping them avoid the kinds of relationship mistakes they have made in the past. Remember that the purpose of fear is to reduce vulnerability to threats. To the extent that Brady, Amanda, and Jack's fears lessen their chances of repeating relationship-threatening behaviors, they therefore serve a purpose. The problem occurs when they let their fears about affection isolate them from the very people who matter most in their lives.

If you avoid expressing as much affection as you wish you received, then it's important to figure out what's holding you back. Perhaps you can identify with the fears experienced by Brady, Amanda, or Jack. You might also have worries or concerns of your own about showing affection. Even fears that seem reasonable or useful can have the negative side effect of keeping you from a promising and fulfilling relationship. To manage your fears properly, therefore, it's first necessary to identify what they are.

Try This

Write a short paragraph about yourself, similar to the paragraphs you just read about Brady, Amanda, and Jack. Focus on any worries or concerns you have that keep you from being more affectionate with others. Strive to describe your fears as clearly and concretely as possible.

Next, Reframe Your Concerns

When people act in problematic ways—such as Amanda's tendency to smother people with affection prematurely—then we can say that their approaches to sharing affection pose a threat to the well-being of a relationship. After damaging or losing relationships as a result of such mistakes, it's understandable that people would be fearful about being affectionate with others. In fact, some people suppress affection not because they have experienced relationship problems themselves, but simply because they can foresee such problems or have known others who have gone through them. Whatever you've been through in your own relationships, perhaps you were able to describe some of your concerns about affection in the Try This paragraph. What's next?

Instead of encouraging you to conquer or eliminate your fears, I'm going to recommend an approach that can help you shift your perspective in both a short-term and long-term way. That approach—called cognitive reframing—begins with paying attention to the language you use to describe your fears.

Take Note of Your Words

Our thoughts and words are intimately connected with our orientation to reality. In the 1960s, psychiatrist Aaron Beck noticed that people who were battling depression tended to have many negative thoughts. If you've ever been clinically depressed or have known someone who was, that's certainly no revelation. Depression leads people to see the world, and especially themselves, in very negative ways. Beck recognized that there was more to the story, however. He proposed that thinking negative thoughts caused people to behave in negative ways that ultimately reinforced their depression. Doing so creates a hard-to-break cycle. The purpose of cognitive reframing is to alter a person's perspective, so that the negative thoughts that encourage undesirable behaviors are replaced with ones that are more positive (or at least, more neutral).

Explained in that way, cognitive reframing may sound simplistic, but the approach is more complex than just getting people to think happy thoughts. It begins with language. For the most part, we think in words—so much so that bilingual people formulate their thoughts differently depending on which language they're using at the time. We also express our thoughts in words, as you did in the paragraph you wrote.

Words, therefore, are more than just a medium for thought. They are the stuff of thought . . . and that implies that you can change your thoughts by altering the words you use to think and express them. That's the basis of cognitive reframing.

To reframe your fears about affection, start by paying attention to the language you use to describe them. As an example, let's suppose that forty-three-year-old Emily wrote the following:

My partner wants me to be a lot more affectionate, but that's just not who I am. I didn't get much affection growing up, so I'm not comfortable being affectionate with people now, especially in public. My partner already knows I love him, so I can't understand why that's not enough.

These sentiments are certainly relatable, but let's focus on the words used to depict them. You may notice, for instance, that much of Emily's language focuses on what *isn't true* instead of what *is true*, such as "I didn't get much affection growing up" and "I'm not comfortable being affectionate." In addition, Emily describes herself in absolute terms when she makes statements such as "that's just not who I am" and "I can't understand why that's not enough."

Reading this paragraph gives you the sense of someone who feels negatively about affectionate behavior and believes she always will. Once we have identified those thoughts, we can work to reframe them by altering how we describe them.

Express Your Thoughts in Less Negative Language

In cognitive reframing, the words you use to express a thought constitute your *frame* for whatever that thought is about. As the name implies, reframing is intended to alter the frame you use to think about an issue. You have seen that the process starts by identifying the characteristics of your frame that are candidates for change. In the previous example, we saw that Emily described her feelings in words that were deficit oriented—that is, focused on what wasn't true instead of what was—and that seemed resistant to change. The next step in the process is to alter the language to make it less negative. Let's illustrate the technique by modifying some parts of Emily's description:

Original statement: *My partner wants me to be a lot more affectionate, but that's just not who I am.*

Reframed statement: *My partner wants me to be a lot more affectionate. I guess he sees something in me that I have yet to see in myself.*

The original statement "that's just not who I am" is framed negatively by focusing on what Emily lacks instead of what she has. It also describes her in absolute terms by implying that she can never be anything other than what she is now. Notice that the reframed statement changes both characteristics—it focuses on what Emily's partner sees in her (instead of what he doesn't see), and it implies that she has the potential to realize and appreciate that aspect of herself (instead of claiming that she can never change).

Here's another example:

Original statement: *I didn't get much affection growing up, so I'm not comfortable being affectionate with people now.*

Reframed statement: *My parents showed me their love by providing for my needs, so expressing affection more directly is a new experience for me.*

Sometimes we focus so much on overt forms of behavior—hugging, kissing, saying "I love you," and the like—that we fail to recognize the many other ways people show us their love. I'll have more to say on this issue in Chapter Nine, but for now, let's recognize that this way of framing affection tends to exclude possibilities rather than include them. In contrast, the reframed statement acknowledges that Emily's parents communicated their affection by providing for her needs, which is worth acknowledging even if she might have wished for more demonstrative displays. Notice also that the original statement again depicts Emily in terms of what isn't true ("I'm not comfortable being affectionate") rather than what is true. The reframed version removes the negativity and also acknowledges that displaying affection (especially publically) is a novel experience for her, one that doesn't necessarily have to be discomforting.

I could rewrite the entire paragraph, but you get the idea. The point of the exercise is to take what is cast in undesirable terms and replace those negative depictions with a neutral or positive alternative.

Try This

Take the paragraph you wrote before and go through it carefully, paying special attention to negative words or depictions. Then, craft a neutral or positive alternative to replace those negative words and depictions. Your goal should not be to change *what you're saying* as much as to reframe *how you're saying it*, bearing in mind that you want your words to imply possibility, create hope, and acknowledge what's good. For example, instead of saying "Hugging my father makes me uncomfortable," try "I'm working on getting used to hugging my father," because that statement expresses hope that you will learn to be comfortable even if you aren't now. Identifying alternative frames is often challenging, but if it stretches your mind and helps you think in new ways, it is worth the effort.

Finally, Operate from Your New Reality

You might be wondering why the focus on thoughts and language matters. At the end of the day, aren't you still giving and receiving the same amount of affection, regardless of how you describe it?

In one sense, you are . . . but in another sense, you may not be. Changing the words you use to think about and describe your situation can ultimately change how you perceive and respond to it. In the earlier example, Emily acknowledged that her parents showed their love by being good providers, even if they didn't hug and kiss her as much as she wanted. By framing her upbringing in that way, Emily replaces the idea that she "didn't get much affection growing up." Her shift in language didn't change her past, but it changed *how she perceived her past,* allowing her to move beyond the idea that she had an affection-deprived childhood.

See, cognitive reframing is about finding—and changing—the negative thoughts that may be impairing your goals. It's less about conquering fear and more about seeing possibility in what appear to be barriers or threats. Reframing can help you find opportunity that was hidden before. In particular, reframing your understanding of the risks of affection can help you turn a problem into an opportunity and make you feel less vulnerable.

The final step, therefore, is to allow your thoughts and actions to be guided by your new frame. That means reminding yourself that you have shifted your thinking, and then behaving as if your reframed understanding of affection is true.

Try This

After reframing your paragraph regarding your concerns about affection, read your new paragraph every morning for a month. As you do, resolve to find at least one way each day to express affection in a manner you would have feared before. Every time you do so, notice the good that comes of it—or at least, the bad that doesn't come of it. At the end of each day, read your paragraph again and pay attention to how your behavior that day reinforced your new understanding of affection.

Cognitive reframing isn't a quick fix for your fears, but by pushing yourself to find different words for them, you can reduce their negative effects on you, freeing you to express more affection to the loved ones in your life.

Stop and Reflect

As I mentioned before, not every suggestion in Part Three of this book will be relevant to every person or every situation. While reading this chapter, you may have felt that you don't have any significant fears about affection that require reframing. That certainly may be true . . . but before proceeding to Chapter Eight, take a moment to reflect on the following questions:

- Do you sometimes think about the most appropriate way to express affection to someone before you express it?
- Have you ever felt affection for someone, but chose not to communicate it because you weren't sure whether he or she felt the same way about you?
- In what situations, if any, has hugging, kissing, or saying "I love you" to someone made you feel vulnerable?

CHAPTER EIGHT

Strategy #2: Invite and Model the Type of Relationship You Seek

When we find ourselves wanting more attention from others, perhaps the simplest route to getting it is just to ask for it. No matter how close our relationships are, our partners and loved ones can't read our minds, so they may not realize we desire more affection than we're receiving.

Some people are inhibited about asking for more affection, even in their close friendships or romantic relationship. They may feel that such a request is petty, or they may think that if they have to ask for affection, then the affection they receive isn't meaningful. On the other hand, some people are so forthright about their desires that they frame their requests as demands, insisting on *more* from their partners.

A helpful alternative to both approaches is to *invite* our partners and friends to show more affection and to *model* the behaviors we especially want.

First, Invite Instead of Demand

Recall our discussion from Chapter Six that being assertive about our needs—such as a need for more direct forms of affection—can be effective, but only if the other person is prepared to hear our request and respond to it. All too often, we fall into the habit of making demands that our loved ones simply aren't willing or able to meet. We can break that pattern, though, if we acknowledge the pitfalls of making demands and learn to *invite* the affection we want, rather than insisting on it.

Beware the Pitfalls of Demanding

To get more affection and undivided attention from those in their lives, some folks take the approach of simply insisting that others express it. Especially with a spouse or long-term friend, some people feel they have the freedom to make their needs known explicitly, such as by saying, *I need you to say you love me more often* or *Please put away your cell phone during lunch so I can have your undivided attention*. Others go so far as to issue an ultimatum such as, *If you don't start showing me more affection, then I want a separation*. For people who desperately want more from their relationships, these tactics can seem efficient . . . but they are rarely effective. Even if they work in the short term, they often fail to bring about long-term change and growth, for at least two reasons.

One of the pitfalls of making such a demand is that it doesn't consider why the partner is unaffectionate or inattentive in the first place. As we've discussed, many barriers can prevent people from showing more affection, even in their closest relationships.

For instance, expressing more affection might feel risky. Some people may fear being emotionally vulnerable, or they may worry about obligating themselves to the relationship in ways they aren't prepared for. That's how Jack, whose story we examined in the previous chapter, feels whenever he starts to get close to someone. Relationship partners might also resist becoming more affectionate if they feel they already show their partners enough affection. In that situation, showing more affection can feel disingenuous, both for the person expressing it and for the one receiving it.

A second pitfall to insisting on more affection is that most people don't enjoy having demands made of them. Especially in close relationships, most of us prefer to be asked to do something instead of told to do it. Being on the receiving end of a demand can feel belittling, regardless of what's being demanded. When one partner is insisting on certain behavior from another, it's easy for the other to become defensive and resist the demand. There's a reason you catch more flies with honey than with vinegar.

Even when people acquiesce to your demands, what they express may not be genuine. Perhaps you remember the story from Chapter Six of Kris, who became insistent on more affection from her fiancé Brad. Brad felt he already expressed an adequate level of affection, and he resented having more insisted of him. To him, an expression such as "I love you" should come organically—he should say it when he actually feels it. On the contrary, expressing love because he's been *told to* would seem almost fraudulent.

Demanding more affection from a partner or attention from a friend may seem like a direct, straightforward way to get it. Much of the time, though, it puts pressure on the partner to communicate in ways that don't feel natural or genuine, which can lead to resentment. Rather than insisting on more affection, a more productive approach is to *invite* it.

Invite Affection

To invite affection means to encourage it from a partner instead of requiring it. That's what Julie, a forty-six-year-old mother of two, decided to try with her best friend Diana. After two decades of friendship, Julie and Diana had become so comfortable with each other that each began taking the other for granted. Both recognized the situation, yet neither really knew what to do about it. Rather than simply grow apart from Diana, Julie decided to reinvest in their friendship, so she began creating opportunities to share close, affectionate time together. For instance, she "kidnapped" Diana one night to take her to a concert she had been eager to see. She arranged a spa day just for the two of them to celebrate Diana's birthday. And, after a particularly difficult week at Diana's job, Julie invited her over for a low-key evening of pizza and wine. Over time, Julie found that these small gestures reminded both Diana and herself of the importance of reconnecting affectionately. Although simple, this strategy encouraged Diana to express her affection for Julie, which strengthened the close friendship they had shared for so many years.

Some may scoff at this advice, believing that "if I have to coax someone into being more affectionate, then it isn't meaningful." Certainly, many of us prefer it when our loved ones initiate affection on their own, and in the exact ways we like. It's useful to remember, though, that our friends and romantic partners can't read our minds. Just as we might encourage someone to be more assertive or more introspective when the situation calls for it, we can invite and encourage him or her to be more expressive of feelings, including feelings of love and affection.

Of course, invitations can be denied . . . and that's one of the reasons why they're more effective than demands. When you're *encouraged* to do something, that implies the option of saying no, which may be critical for people who feel restricted from showing affection for whatever reason. By issuing an invitation instead of a demand, you send the implicit message that the other person has permission to decide whether—and how—to respond. This can take much of the pressure off of people who are uncomfortable showing affection because it creates a safe space for them to do so.

Inviting affection therefore takes a bit more patience. Sometimes people will fail to notice our invitation, and sometimes they will decline it. When an invitation is declined, the impatient person reissues the request in the form of a demand. However, remaining patient in such situations implies that our partner has permission to make his or her own decisions, and that we will honor them. Creating that sense of safety and autonomy for our partner may not bring about immediate results like demanding something might, but it is more likely to attract those behaviors in a genuine and longer-lasting way.

Try This

Think of the one behavior—hugging, undivided attention, more time spent together, or so on—that you most desire more frequently from a friend or loved one. Then, formulate two strategies for inviting that behavior. If you want more time with a friend, for instance, choose the appropriate moment and say, "I'd love to spend time together next week if you're free." If it's kisses from your romantic partner you crave, give three kiss-coupons as a gift. Simple as these tactics sound, they communicate to your loved one that you would enjoy these expressions without framing your request as a demand.

Next, Model the Behaviors You Desire

As we've noted throughout this book, not everyone feels comfortable giving or receiving attention and affection. The tactics we just explored can invite certain behaviors, but some people will need extra encouragement. Perhaps your loved ones *want* to be more expressive with you, but they aren't sure how to do so. They may not know what kinds of affectionate expressions you enjoy most, or they may have tried showing their affection in ways you've overlooked, making them feel unsuccessful. Whatever the specifics, using a tactic called *modeling* can reinforce your invitations.

Understand the Purpose of Modeling

Modeling means displaying the behaviors you want from others, and it is a fundamental strategy for teaching. The principle behind modeling is that we can learn how to do something successfully by watching other people do it. When I was growing up, I learned how to make oatmeal raisin cookies not by reading and following a recipe but by watching my mother make them and imitating what she did. I noticed, for instance, that she sprayed the cookie sheet with oil before baking a batch, and I discovered that doing so kept my cookies from sticking to the sheet. In the same vein, I learned to stand during the Pledge of Allegiance, with my right hand over my heart, not by having someone teach me that specifically but by watching what my teacher did and copying her. We might call this strategy *teaching by example*.

Modeling isn't the only way we learn, of course. We acquire knowledge through instruction, such as learning how to drive by taking a driver's ed class. We also learn from our own experiences, such as discovering through trial and error which times of the day are busiest at the gym. Modeling is one strategy among many for imparting information, but it can be especially effective at teaching appropriate patterns of behavior, and not just for children. I was already out of graduate school the first time I visited China, where I quickly realized I didn't always know the appropriate ways to behave in various situations. When visiting a fast food restaurant, for example, I expected to line up with other customers in front of each open cash register—but by observing others, I quickly learned that crowding in front of the registers and pushing your way to the front was the expected behavior. No one told me that was the custom, and I hadn't experienced it before, yet I learned it by imitating the behavior that others were modeling.

Through modeling, we can learn not only what behaviors are possible, but also what works best in a given situation. Had someone explained before my China visit that people at McDonald's would push and shove me aside in order to reach the counter, I would have considered that behavior to be malicious and rude . . . and I would have expected others to show disapproval for people who acted that way. On the contrary, observing the behavior myself taught me that it was not only *accepted* and *expected* in that social situation but actually *effective*. It worked, and largely because no one considered it malicious or rude the way I otherwise would have.

Modeling did its job in that situation by teaching me a pattern of behavior that garnered positive results.

Model the Behaviors You Enjoy

Modeling can be just as effective when you're trying to boost your relationship with someone. The strategy is to let your partner observe you enacting the very behaviors that you want more of from him or her.

As an example, let's consider Valeria, aged fifty-one, who has been married to her husband Matías for nearly thirty years. Valeria wishes Matías would tell her he loves her more often, but she believes that doing so makes him feel vulnerable. To encourage the behavior she seeks and to show him the positive effects it can have, she lets him hear her saying "I love you" to other important people in her life, including her sisters, her close friends, and their own son, Gabriel. She wants Matías to see how comfortable she is expressing herself this way, and how happy it makes her to hear "I love you" from others in return.

Valeria understands that her husband finds it daunting to express his love verbally. If she simply started saying "I love you" to him, therefore, he would feel obligated to say the same back—and although that would give her the affectionate expression she wants, she realizes it won't help Matías become comfortable saying it on his own. To model the behavior in a less threatening way, Valeria writes "I love you" on a Post-it note and leaves it on Matías's workbench. That allows him to see the expression being directed at himself without feeling put on the spot to reciprocate.

The point of modeling isn't to treat your friend or partner like a child. It's to lead by example, by demonstrating—in nonthreatening ways—the very behaviors you enjoy and desire.

Try This

When you and your partner are around loved ones, such as during holidays and graduations, let your partner see you expressing affection to your relatives and friends. If it feels natural to do so, encourage and invite your partner to communicate affection to you at the same time—otherwise, focus on letting him or her observe your own affectionate behaviors with other important people.

Finally, Be Patient and Reinforce Positive Change

The one advantage that demanding something has going for it is efficiency. Unless friends or partners want to hurt your feelings, start a fight, or precipitate a separation, they will generally acquiesce and provide what you ask. To the extent that those expressions are coerced instead of voluntary, however, they may be less than fully genuine, and may even engender resentment from the person who offered them. Although demanding is efficient, it isn't a recipe for long-term relational growth.

The alternative of inviting and modeling desired behaviors is more likely to attract genuine affection, but it requires patience. Not everyone responds to invitations in the same way, nor learns from modeling to the same degree. These are long-term strategies that require patient implementation to succeed. That patience may be difficult for some people who feel they have waited long enough for a more attentive friend or affectionate partner, but it is essential for real and sustained growth.

As loved ones respond to invitations and modeling, a useful tactic is to encourage their behavior through positive reinforcement. In behavioral psychology, *positive reinforcement* means responding to a desired change in behavior with rewards. It is an integral part of training, or *conditioning*, for both animals and humans. For example, dog trainers provide a small treat whenever a dog sits on command. The treat serves as a reward, encouraging the specific behavior that led to it (sitting on command). Similarly, a mother might promise ice cream if her children clean their rooms within a specified time period. In that case, the ice cream rewards and reinforces the behavior Mom wants. Decades of research, dating back to the work of behaviorist B.F. Skinner, have shown the effectiveness of positive reinforcement for producing behavior change.

I'm not suggesting plying your loved ones with ice cream or doggie treats whenever they show you affection. Nonetheless, it's useful to acknowledge when your invitation is accepted. In those instances, expressions of praise and gratitude can work very well to reward the behavior and reinforce its likelihood of continuing. We all enjoy having our efforts acknowledged and appreciated, so when your loved ones respond to your invitation and modeling with the behaviors you desire, providing positive reinforcement is an effective strategy for encouraging continued growth.

Try This

As you model affectionate behavior for a loved one and invite him or her to express the same to you, take note of the person's progress, and praise it. For instance, Julie noticed that Diana hugged her (without being asked or encouraged to do so) after an evening of dinner and drinks together. In reply, Julie said, "Thank you for the hug . . . I really loved that!" Simple expressions of praise such as this convey the message that you notice the other person's efforts and appreciate them. Hugging Julie was a small gesture on Diana's part, but Julie's positive feedback reinforced her efforts and encouraged a more substantive affectionate gesture the next time.

Stop and Reflect

Before you proceed to Chapter Nine, take a moment to consider these questions:

- In your close relationships, what can you do to invite attentive and affectionate behavior?
- How do you already model the affection displays you wish to receive from others? How can you model them more overtly?
- In what ways are you comfortable encouraging and reinforcing positive change in your loved ones?

Strategy #3: Recognize Diversity in Affection Displays

People who wish that others were more affectionate sometimes think too narrowly about what affection is and how it can be expressed. I may want more affection from my father, for instance, but I might think only of behaviors such as hugging or saying "I love you" when making that desire known. Consequently, I would notice and give him credit for increasing only those specific behaviors.

Many of us have particular forms of affection that we prefer, whether it's kissing, handholding, or exchanging meaningful gifts. Whether as a result of our culture, our family upbringing, our personality, or even our biology, we may welcome and respond to some affection displays more than others. It is certainly fine to have those preferences and to make them known. At the same time, it is helpful to remember that affection can come in multiple forms. Just as people vary in how much affection they need, they also differ in how they show their affection. To get more affection in your life, therefore, it pays to consider the expressions you are already receiving but may be overlooking.

As we'll see in this chapter, this is particularly relevant advice for people in opposite-sex relationships, whether with lovers, friends, or family members. You probably acknowledge that women and men often perceive their relational worlds differently, and that is certainly true with affection. So, even if you want more of a specific type of behavior, it helps to recognize that your partner may already be showing affection in ways you're missing.

First, Understand That People Vary

Everyone needs affection, and I believe virtually everyone is born with the capacity to show it, as well. That doesn't mean we all express affection in the same ways, though. Rather, we vary from person to person, and from group to group, in the behaviors we use to convey our love and in the types of expressions we prefer to receive from others. When we aren't attuned to those differences, we miss out on affection that is expressed to us, causing us to consider ourselves more affection deprived than we actually are.

Pay Attention to Different Styles of Affection

As we have already discussed, affection can be communicated in a variety of forms. We sometimes convey love verbally, such as by saying "I love you" or writing it in a card. On other occasions, we prefer nonverbal gestures, such as kissing and handholding, or socially supportive behaviors, such as doing a friend a favor. We usually decide how to express affection based on the type of situation we're in and the kind of relationship we have with the person receiving it. In fact, it's quite common for people to be more open and overt with their affection in certain situations and relation-ships than in others.

Affectionate behavior also varies from person to person. Each of us has ways of communicating love and support that feel more comfortable than others. For example, consider Kaitlyn and Steve, who have been married for eleven years. Kaitlyn is a highly expressive person. Whether she's feeling joyful, angry, disgusted, or nervous, she is comfortable expressing her emotions verbally to people around her. When it comes to the affection she feels for Steve, their children, or her close friends and relatives, she is also highly demonstrative. She enjoys the physical contact of hugging, touching, kissing, and holding hands, and is rarely hesitant to express her feelings of warmth, love, and empathy in that manner.

In comparison, Steve is much more private and reserved. As Kaitlyn sometimes says, "He's a difficult man to read." For the most part, he prefers to keep his emotions—whether positive or negative—to himself. He is comfortable kissing, holding hands, and saying "I love you" when Kaitlyn initiates those behaviors, but he almost never initiates them on his own.

None of that means that Steve doesn't feel as much affection for Kaitlyn as she feels for him. He absolutely does . . . he simply has a different style of showing it. Steve tends to convey his love through the things he does for Kaitlyn and their family, rather than through direct verbal or nonverbal expressions. If asked how he shows Kaitlyn affection, he would say that it's by making sure her car is well maintained, ensuring that the lawn and garden always look nice when she's planning a family gathering, feeding their cat and three dogs every morning, and seeing to all the neces-sary home repairs before she even becomes aware of them.

Although Steve appreciates Kaitlyn's more expressive style of communicating affection, his own style is to convey his feelings *through his actions* rather than through words or gestures. To him, tending to his wife's instrumental needs is a more valuable contribution—and a more meaningful expression of his love—than giving hugs or cards. For her part, Kaitlyn recognized early in their relationship that this was Steve's style, and so she interprets and appreciates his work as a genuine expression of his affection for her.

Often, however, these more active, instrumental ways of conveying affection go unnoticed because they don't take the more emotionally expressive, demonstrative forms that many people associate with affection. For the person providing them, however, they are no less genuine and meaningful than a kiss or an "I love you."

Account for Sex Differences in Affectionate Behavior

Either women or men can prefer Steve's instrumental, hands-on approach to communicating affection. There's a great deal of overlap in the styles men and women use, with some men being emotionally demonstrative and some women favoring a more instrumental approach. That's a matter of each person's individual personality. Years of research have confirmed, however, that men are more likely to prefer Steve's approach. Besides the individual difference between people, that is, there is also a group difference based on sex.

In several of my own studies, for instance, I have asked adults to describe how they usually show affection to their loved ones. For most people, it's a mix of expressive behaviors (such as hugging and saying "I love you") and instrumental behaviors (such as changing the oil in the car). Few of us are equally likely to use both strategies, though—we generally prefer one approach to the other. As we've discussed, there is person-to-person variation in what we favor, but there are also two important sex differences. The first is that *men are more likely than women to express affection through instrumental behaviors*. That reflects the difference between Kaitlyn and Steve, for instance. Second, *men are more likely to use instrumental behaviors than they are to use expressive behaviors*, which is why Steve prefers to show his love through an auto tune-up than a Hallmark card.

Both of these differences are heightened in people's relationships with others of the same sex. For example, when I've compared brother-brother and sister-sister pairs, or even male-male and female-female friendships, the differences between women and men become even more pronounced. The brothers are very likely to use instrumental behaviors versus expressive to show affection, and the sisters are very likely to use expressive behaviors. They are still present in opposite-sex relationships, however, including many marriages.

I can't say for certain why men and women favor different styles. It may be akin to a cultural difference, if one can think of masculinity and femininity as reflecting different cultural expectations for behavior. At least in North America, the "culture of masculinity" encourages men to be responsible for tasks such as car care and home repair, so it often feels natural to men (and even to women who identify as masculine) to show their love for others in such active, care-providing ways. At the same time, the masculine culture discourages the expression of feelings in more overt ways, such as verbally or via direct gestures such as hugging. We might say exactly the opposite about the "culture of femininity." To the extent that North American societies raise girls and boys with different expectations about appropriate behavior—including affectionate behavior—they create what are akin to separate cultures for masculine and feminine people.

The sex differences in preferred styles of affection may also have a biological basis. In recent years, scientists have found that overt behaviors such as kissing and hugging can affect women and men differently at the hormonal level. Some researchers have argued that women are more affectionate than men because they get a greater reward in the form of feel-good hormones such as oxytocin and dopamine. Over time, people become conditioned to repeat behaviors that induce a feel-good response, so if that response is more common for women than men, this may also explain why expressive styles of communicating affection are also more characteristic of women.

As with many behaviors, a combination of social and biological causes may underlie the sex difference in styles of affection. No matter the causes, the important thing is to notice whether that difference is present in your own relationships.

Try This

Identifying another person's style of communicating affection includes recognizing the ways in which you differ from each other. Take a moment to think about yourself and about your spouse or partner. Make a short list of the ways in which you differ from each other *in terms of your communication*. What kinds of communication do you each value? When are you more likely to talk, and when do you prefer communicating in nonverbal ways?

Notice Forms of Affection You Already Receive

Your friends or romantic partners may have tried communicating affection to you in ways that felt natural to them, but were not interpreted as such by you. Especially for men, affection is shown more through actions than through words or gestures. Hugging or saying "I love you" may seem a bit effortless—and therefore, less meaningful—to some men, whereas expending effort for your benefit is a genuinely affectionate message to them. If you want more affection in your life, therefore, it makes sense to notice and acknowledge every bit of affection you're already receiving.

Become Aware of Instrumental Affectionate Behaviors

I used the term *instrumental* to describe Steve's more active, task-oriented style of conveying affection because his efforts center on tasks that are instrumental—that is, necessary and useful—to his daily life with Kaitlyn. Although either men or women can prefer an instrumental affection style, it tends to be more characteristic of men. In this discussion, therefore, I will use masculine pronouns and ask you to think about what the men in your life do, although instrumental forms of affection can also come from women.

Having said that, I want to encourage you to become aware of the ways your friend or loved one shows you affection through instrumental gestures. Perhaps a friend goes to a networking event with you so you're not there alone. Maybe your spouse comes home early to cook you dinner, or spends his Saturday cleaning out the attic because he knows you'd like to use that space. Instrumental gestures of affection can be as large as installing a new furnace in the fall so you'll have warmth during the winter and as small as sending a text message to see how a stressful doctor's appointment went.

It's easy to dismiss these actions as "stuff he should be doing anyway . . . what does he want, a medal?" To him, though, these may be just as genuine an expression of affection as kissing and handholding are to you.

The same is often true when he's with his buddies. Many men don't hug or say "I love you" to their friends. Those behaviors may not feel natural to them, yet that doesn't mean they don't have genuine feelings of affection for each other. Consider thirty-year-old Paul, who has known his best friends Dale and Matt since junior high. All three men are comfortable expressing affection directly with their wives . . . but with each other, their affection takes more instrumental forms. Two years ago, Matt and Paul both took vacation time from their jobs to help Dale install a new roof. Last spring, when Paul's wife suffered a miscarriage, Dale picked up Paul's son from daycare and brought him home for a sleepover with his own kids, so that Paul and his wife could have time together. Matt, Paul, and Dale may not voice the words "I love you" to each other, but their actions convey that message loudly and clearly. If asked, they would probably say they don't feel a great need to express their affection verbally, because they show how they feel about each other through their actions.

Acknowledge Instrumental Affectionate Behaviors

It's one thing to become aware of how your loved ones express affection to you. A second and equally important step is to acknowledge those expressions.

In my own research, many people—almost all of them men—have told me that their biggest relationship frustration is that their gestures of love go unacknowledged. For them, it's more than a matter of having their work (whether tending to the car, cutting the lawn, or whatever) appreciated. It's that they wish their significant others would interpret that work as the expression of love that it is. Take a moment to consider whether that is true in your own relationship. To the extent that it is, several negative effects can follow.

The most immediate effect is that he feels his efforts to show love are invisible, and therefore unimportant. Any of us can imagine (or perhaps, remember) sending someone an affectionate card or gift that goes unacknowledged. Understandably, we would feel slighted, perhaps emotionally hurt, and discouraged from sending similar expressions in the future. When men's efforts to show affection through instrumental gestures go *repeatedly* unacknowledged, they feel slighted, hurt, and discouraged on an ongoing basis.

A second negative effect is that repeated dismissals of their efforts make men feel like failures at affection. What's worse, their partners may feel the same way. It's true that men aren't as demonstrative of their affection as women are, on average. In fact, men are less demonstrative than women of many emotions. That's not just a stereotype; it's an accurate assessment, according to research. It's also accurate to say that many women find this frustrating and wish their husbands or boyfriends would be more expressive. It's fine to wish for that, even to encourage that, but it is useful to remember that men aren't failures at communication simply because they communicate differently than you do. It's understandable why they would feel that way, however, when their typical ways of expressing themselves go unappreciated.

Finally, failing to acknowledge men's more instrumental style can have the effect of locking women into a narrow, limited concept of how love can be expressed. If women take the position, whether consciously or subconsciously, that only behaviors such as hugging, kissing, or saying "I love you" *count* as affectionate, then they paradoxically limit their own options for expressing affection as well as the options of men. To do so actually belies women's lived experience. Many women, that is, intuitively understand that instrumental favors done by their sisters or close friends convey feelings of affection and love, even if they don't recognize the same in men's behaviors. To fail to acknowledge the broad range of affectionate gestures *limits both women and men* to a narrow concept of what affection is and how it can be communicated.

Even if these problems sound complicated, their solution is simple. As you become more adept at identifying instrumental forms of affection, make a point to acknowledge and appreciate them. Perhaps you do so verbally, by telling him how much it means to you that he takes care of instrumental needs without being asked. You might say you appreciate how he looks out for your comfort and safety, which makes you feel loved. You can also convey these messages nonverbally, such as by responding to his instrumental expressions with more demonstrative expressions of your own. Offering a hug and kiss after he fixes the leaky roof can show appreciation as well as words can. However it feels natural to do, acknowledging and appreciating instrumental forms of affection can go a long way toward addressing and preventing the problems I've discussed, making men feel their affectionate gestures are valued.

Try This

Try to think like your spouse or partner for a moment, and consider his or her perspective on your relationship. How does he or she naturally show affection to you and to other loved ones? Make a list of the ways—whether they are expressive or instrumental—in which your spouse or partner shows you affection, paying particular attention to any ways you don't typically recognize or acknowledge. Then, describe three ways in which you could acknowledge and express appreciation for those behaviors more than you already do.

Be Willing to Self-Reflect

For any of us whose partners are less affectionate than we wish, it can be easy to assign all the blame to them. In my work, I often hear the claim that "I've tried everything to get him to be more affectionate, and he simply refuses." When I hear people say that, I realize they may have tried *everything they can think of.* In my experience, though, it is usually the case that everything they've tried has been directed at changing their partner, without considering the importance of changing themselves.

The strategy described in this chapter is a perfect example. If we want more affection, it helps to expand our own mindset about what affection is and how it can be expressed, so that we're acknowledging all the affection we currently receive. Notice that this strategy is mostly self-focused; it isn't about changing your partner so much as it is about changing yourself.

That requires willingness to self-reflect and to admit that your lack of attention or affection may not be entirely his fault. The other person may very well be showing affection in ways you simply aren't noticing—so to change that requires self-reflection.

Understandably, people are often apprehensive about self-reflecting. It is easier cognitively—and certainly safer emotionally—to focus attention on what others do wrong than to admit and address shortcomings of your own. There's certainly no shame in feeling hesitant about self-reflection. Even if it's discomforting, however, it is nonetheless valuable, both for individuals and their relationships.

It's also essential for adopting the strategy described in this chapter. Whether you feel highly affection deprived or not, taking stock of all the affection you receive—including the forms you're overlooking right now—requires thinking carefully about how you notice your partner's behavior and then changing how you think and act. All of that is effortful, much more so than simply blaming the other person. The effort of self-reflection is worth it, however, not only for romantic relationships but for all relationships in which you receive instrumental affectionate gestures.

Try This

On two or three separate occasions, find a place free of noise and distraction where you can reflect on yourself and the relationship in question. Start by making a list of the ways you already show affection comfortably to your friend or partner. Being self-reflective doesn't mean being self-critical, so let yourself acknowledge what you already do well in your relationship. Next, if the other person is less attentive or affectionate than you would like, ask yourself—honestly and without judgment—what part you play in this lack. For example, do you give him or her credit only for the particular affectionate behaviors you prefer? Finally, think about what role you could play in creating a more affectionate relationship, and ask yourself honestly whether that role should include acknowledging and appreciating the other person's style of expressing affection, even if it is different from your own.

In many relationships, increasing the affection you receive is partly a function of noticing and appreciating forms of affection you are currently overlooking. We all overlook gestures of love from time to time, but we grow in our relationships—and we feel less deprived of affection—when we encourage ourselves to identify, acknowledge, and show appreciation for them, even if they come in active, instrumental forms.

Stop and Reflect

Learning to notice and appreciate a wider variety of affectionate expressions takes time, effort, and self-reflection. Before moving on to Chapter Ten, give some thought to these queries:

- Why do women and men so often have different styles of expressing affection? Is either style inherently better than the other?
- Besides the examples mentioned in this chapter, what other instrumental behaviors reflect affection in your own relationships?
- What can you do to show your appreciation for a wider range of affectionate expressions?

CHAPTER TEN

Strategy #4: Nurture a Variety of Affectionate Relationships

One reason people have less affection than they want in their lives is that they expect one person to fulfill all of their attention and affection needs. As we've discussed, we start out our lives looking to our parents—especially our mothers—to meet our needs for affection. There's nothing wrong with that when we're infants, but as we mature, we sometimes make the mistake of continuing to expect one specific person to provide us with all the affection we desire. That person is often our romantic partner, but it can also be a parent, another family member, or a friend. No matter the specifics, expecting one person to meet all of our affection needs is unrealistic. To invite more affection, it is helpful to cast a wider net. That process starts by taking stock of the expectations you currently hold. It then involves nurturing affection in a wider variety of relationships.

First, Take Stock of Your Expectations

We sometimes make impractical and unreasonable expectations of others without realizing we're doing so. To break that pattern, we have to examine our expectations carefully to determine how they are limiting us in our relationships . . . and importantly, we must do so in an honest, open manner.

Determine How Your Expectations Limit You

When it comes to managing your personal relationships, you may have very realistic expectations. Recall our earlier discussion of attachment security, which is a person's ability to trust and count on his or her significant relationships with family, friends, and romantic partners. Your relationship with your primary caregiver imprints on you a style of attaching to others. If your style reflects a high level of security, that means you feel comfortable trusting other people and having them trust you, and you don't worry about your loved ones either smothering you or abandoning you. As a result, you'll tend to have sensible, realistic expectations about the affection you receive from other people. You generally know how much affection to anticipate from others, and you don't usually feel deprived.

Feeling secure in your attachments is a blessing that many people don't share. Instead, many have insecure styles of attachment, meaning they don't feel as confident in the strength of their relationship bonds. As I explained in Chapter Seven, insecure attachments come in three primary forms:

- Those with a *fearful style* want intimacy with others, but intimacy also scares them. When they meet someone new, they typically let the relationship get only so close before backing away.
- People with a *preoccupied style*, however, rarely feel like they get as much love, intimacy, and affection from others as

they want. They worry constantly that others don't *really* love them, even if they say they do, and that loved ones will eventually leave them. To prevent being abandoned, they frequently smother loved ones with affection and put enormous pressure on others to reciprocate.

- People with a *dismissive style* don't feel a strong drive to develop intimacy with others. They're generally uncomfortable depending on other people or having others depend on them, preferring instead to be left alone.

Expecting one person to meet all of your affection needs is problematic for a number of reasons. For one, it puts an enormous amount of pressure on the other person. Whether the relationship is romantic, platonic, or familial, few people probably enjoy that level of pressure, and those who don't are understandably likely to rebel. If you expect a specific person to provide you with all of the love, intimacy, and affection that you want, that person often feels so pressured that your relationship might fail. This might only confirm your fear that others would leave you, but in truth it's the *unrealistic expectations that were driving them off.* Thus, people who take this approach often create a self-fulfilling prophecy, fearing abandonment while actually facilitating it with their own behaviors.

Besides putting enormous pressure on people, expecting them to meet our affection needs sets them up for failure. No matter how much they care about you, most people simply aren't capable of singlehandedly providing a person with all the love he or she wants. That's doubly true if you desire a great deal of affection in your life, as many of us do. Even people who do have the capacity to fulfill your needs often cannot do so indefinitely. The unavoidable results of your expectations, then, are failure and disappointment, which is never a recipe for long-term relationship success.

A third shortcoming of putting all our affection eggs in one basket is that we deny ourselves the chance to experience love in a wider swath of relationships. The more pressure I put on one person to make me happy, the less opportunity I have to find happiness in a variety of bonds. Even if we've found someone we consider our soulmate, we still benefit from having a variety of close relationships with people who complement different aspects of our personality. I'll have more to say on this later in the chapter, because nurturing a wider diversity of relationships can be a key strategy for finding more affection in your life.

Be Honest with Yourself

Taking stock of your expectations is an important first step in making them more realistic, but it's a somewhat useless exercise if you aren't honest about what you find. Of course, not everyone finds it easy to self-reflect. Having a good, long look at ourselves can be intimidating because we're often unsure what we'll see. What's more, many of us are hesitant to admit having beliefs or expectations that are unreasonable. These tendencies serve to protect our egos and fortify our self-esteem, but they often prevent honest self-assessment.

Psychologists say we have a *self-serving bias* that makes us eager to acknowledge our strengths but reluctant to recognize our weaknesses. Consider Ashley, currently in her third year as an accounting student at a large state university. Ashley usually makes good grades in her math and business courses, which she attributes to her hard work and her aptitude with all things numeric. In her mind, she gets high marks in those classes because she earns them and deserves them. Like most students, though, she is also required to take courses in the humanities. Her performance in those classes is much more hit-or-miss. When she makes good grades in a humanities course, she again attributes it to her hard work. When she performs poorly, however, she usually blames it on poor instruction or an unfair grading system.

In other words, Ashley believes her successes are earned, whereas her failures are someone else's fault. That bias supports her self-esteem and protects her from having to admit that she earns her poor grades as well as her good ones. Most people who know Ashley, however, see right through this ruse, recognizing that she simply doesn't make the effort necessary to earn high marks in courses she doesn't enjoy.

It's often easy to see the self-serving bias at work in other people. It's far more difficult to recognize it in yourself. To benefit from self-reflection, though, you have to be willing to view yourself as you are, not just as you wish to be. That's as true for your expectations about relationships as for any other important domain in your life. When you take stock of your expectations for affection—and particularly as you consider how they may be unrealistic and self-limiting—you must do so with a mind that is open to recognizing both your problems and your potential.

Try This

One of the glitches we encounter when reflecting on our expectations is that we confuse them with our desires. Sometimes our expectations are unreasonable because we don't separate *what we want* from *what we can reasonably expect*. Take time to think carefully about one of your close friendships, and then draft a list with two columns, one representing what you desire from that person in terms of affection and the other representing what you feel is reasonable to expect. In the first column, for instance, you might write "I want to see her four times a week," whereas in the second column, you may write "I can reasonably expect to see her twice a week." Paying attention to any differences can help you clarify your expectations.

Next, Nurture Affection in a Wider Variety of Relationships

Suppose you expect your affection needs to be met by one source—such as your spouse or children. Let's suppose further that you continue to want more affection than you get. We could conclude from those suppositions that your current strategy isn't working optimally and that it's time to try something new. My advice isn't to withdraw from the people you currently expect to meet your needs. Rather, it's to stop expecting all your affection to come from one source and to invite affection from a wider variety of relationships, both existing and new.

Find Affection in Existing Relationships

When you're trying to nurture affection in a wider range of relationships, it helps to start with relationships you already have. Even if you have pinned most of your hopes for affection on a particular person, you probably have other important relationships that can develop into valuable and reliable sources of affection.

You might remember Anna, whose story we encountered in Chapter Six. She realized that no matter how much she wanted affection from her mother, she was unlikely to get it because her mother simply wasn't an affectionate person. As Anna explained, "When I did not get the affection I needed from my mother I felt rejected, unloved, sad, [and] it was hard to cope with bad things that happened. I felt very isolated and alone."

It would have been easy for Anna to expect her mother to meet her affection needs, even though she realized that was unlikely to happen. She didn't make that mistake, though. Instead, she nurtured a broader range of existing relationships—including with her children and her mother-in-law—as sources of the affection she desired in her life.

In Anna's case, the person whose affection she most wanted—her mother—was simply incapable of providing that affection. In other situations, though, the person from whom we want love and affection does provide it, just not at a level that is sufficient to meet our needs completely. Consider Elena, a forty-year-old wife and mother of three. She and her husband Terry have a close and affectionate relationship, but no matter how much affection she receives from Terry, Elena always wants and expects more. Unlike Anna, therefore, she is getting some affection from the person she expects it from; it's just never enough.

If you identify with either Anna or Elena, think about the resources already available to you. Consider your friends, relatives, coworkers, and others with whom you share a positive relationship. As you think of people you already know, consider whom you would like to know better. In which relationships do you want to invest? Relationships grow when they are nurtured, and by nurturing some of the relationships you already have, you can find more of the affection that is missing in your life. Suppose you want to become closer to a coworker. Consider an activity you both enjoy, such as going to a wine tasting, running in a charity race, or watching a horror movie marathon. Invite him or her to share such an activity with you. Research—as well as everyday experience—tells us that we feel closer to people when we share enjoyable activities with them. Make sure you minimize outside distractions so you can pay as much attention as possible to your coworker. While you're together, ask your coworker questions about him- or herself. Most of us enjoy telling stories about our lives, so focusing your attention on your coworker—instead of talking only about yourself—can heighten the closeness he or she feels toward you. I realize this advice sounds simple, but some of our most complex interpersonal problems have simple solutions.

Find Affection in New Relationships

For a variety of reasons, nurturing more affectionate relationships with people we already know may help, but that strategy alone may not be sufficient to meet our affection needs. Perhaps you've just moved to a new city, for instance, and you don't yet have a strong social network in place. Or maybe you have focused so much energy expecting affection from your spouse or partner that you haven't nurtured other close relationships in your life. Or you may have good relationships with friends or relatives, but their affection isn't making you feel fully complete.

In those situations, it helps to diversify your strategy and look for affection in new relationships. I don't necessarily mean new romantic relationships, although you may decide that such a move is warranted. Rather, I mean new *social* relationships, whether with friends, neighbors, coworkers, or others.

You might recall Juan Mann from this book's introduction. At the start of his story, he had recently returned to his native Australia and was feeling lonely, disconnected, and without the level of affection that he needed. His solution—to begin offering hugs on the street—was effective, if a bit drastic. If you're equally bold and wish to stage a Free Hugs event, then more power to you—but you needn't take such dramatic measures in order to benefit from Juan Mann's experience.

The lesson in his story is to be proactive about finding new affectionate relationships instead of believing you can't develop them or don't deserve them. Finding new relationships isn't always easy. That's especially true for adults, whose lives often revolve around routines that restrict their interactions to the same range of people. Routines have their place, but they can easily keep us in a rut with respect to the people we know and see.

The solution is to consider activities that provide natural avenues for interacting and developing trust with others. Here's a short list of some potential activities:

- Sign up for a benefit walk
- Join an investment club
- Take a public speaking class
- Attend services at a new church or synagogue
- Join a gym or start a lunch-hour exercise group
- Throw a party where every invitee brings a companion you don't already know
- Volunteer at a hospital, a school, or an animal shelter
- If you're bold enough, host your own Free Hugs event

Those activities are diverse, but they have an important element in common: Each can offer the opportunity to meet and develop relationships with people outside your normal circle. Obviously, you won't develop close, affectionate relationships with everyone you meet. You may with some people, though, and nurturing those can go a long way toward increasing the overall amount of affection you have in your life.

Widening our social circle in search of affection can be a useful strategy, but it can also make us feel as though we've given up on the person whose affection we crave. Suppose you realize you have expected your spouse to meet all or most of your affection needs, and then to remedy that situation, you work on developing new friendships. Doing so might make you feel like you're admitting defeat in your marriage, as though you're giving up on your spouse's ability to provide affection. That's an understandable feeling. What you're really doing, though, isn't *giving up on your spouse*—it's *removing the pressure of your unrealistic expectations*. It's realizing that you are demanding too much from one relationship and rectifying that problem, not declaring your marriage a failure.

Try This

Plan an evening or weekend to spend—uninterrupted and without your significant other—with another close person in your life, such as a friend or a sibling. Choose someone with whom you want to rebuild or strengthen your connection. Focus on appreciating and enjoying that person and that relationship during your time together. As you're able, do the same with others. Appreciate the affection you share with these people, rather than focusing on how much *more* affection you may want with your partner.

Finally, as you're thinking about new affectionate relationships, don't forget that pets are among the most affectionate companions, and relationships with pets are especially therapeutic. Petting a cat or dog has stress-alleviating effects, such as lowering your blood pressure, and research shows that it also reduces the pet's blood pressure, as well. If having a pet in your home isn't feasible, consider volunteering to walk dogs for the Humane Society or another local pet shelter. That gives you a chance to make new friends of both the animal and the human variety. If you don't have time to volunteer, just stop by sometime and pet the animals available for adoption. Many of them are as starved for affection as you may be!

Finally, Protect Your Existing Relationships While Developing New Ones

As I previously alluded to, widening your circle of close relationships is useful for many reasons, not the least of which is that it opens new avenues for sharing affection. To be successful, though, that strategy has to be accompanied by a sufficient level of care over your existing relationships to ensure that they aren't neglected as you broaden your relational horizons.

Consider Dan and Tammy, who have been married for twenty-two years. Tammy realized some time ago that she didn't get as much affection as she wanted—and that part of the reason was that she looked only to Dan to fulfill her affection desires. To invite more affection in her life, she began nurturing new close relationships. Unfortunately, she did so without considering the effect of her actions on Dan.

As Tammy spent more and more time with her new friends, Dan started feeling neglected. He had been trying to express more affection to Tammy because he knew that's what she wanted . . . but even as he became more demonstrative of his feelings, she was around less and less to receive his gestures of affection. He came home early from work one afternoon to make her a special dinner, only to find she had already made plans with two of her new friends to see a concert together, not returning home until late in the evening. Even though Dan can take care of himself, he felt that Tammy was investing in their marriage less and less.

As time went by, Dan's feelings migrated from neglect to jealousy. Among Tammy's circle of new friends were several men, some of whom she seemed quite fond of. On at least one occasion, she went for drinks after work with one of the men. Dan believed that Tammy loved him and was committed to their marriage, but the more time she spent with other men—even though it was only social, never romantic or sexual—the more jealous he became. Finally, Dan reached a point where he thought Tammy was starting to give up on him. Even though she never actually felt that way, Dan perceived that she did.

Dan and Tammy's situation illustrates an important lesson about widening your circle of close relationships: Even as you do so, it is important to protect the close relationships you already have, especially your marriage or partnership. Tammy certainly had the best of intentions when she started making new friends, but she would have done better to nurture affection from her existing relationships *as well as* from new ones. Without realizing it, she had presumed that Dan wouldn't feel put off or threatened by her new friendships. They were, after all, only friendships—

and Dan's previous lack of affection hinted that he didn't care that much about what Tammy did. As it turned out, Tammy's presumption was wrong, and it led to some hurt feelings and dissatisfaction in her marriage.

None of this is meant to suggest that spouses or partners—whether women or men—don't have a *right* to befriend other people and share affection with them. If the marriage or relationship is to last, however, the new friends cannot be treated as surrogates for the partner. If your spouse or partner is uncomfortable with, or feels threatened by, the new relationships you are forming, then it's important to deal openly with those feelings instead of making faulty presumptions, as Tammy did. The bottom line is that existing close relationships—whether they are with romantic partners, family members, or friends—deserve protection, not neglect, even as you are broadening your circle of affection.

Try This

Invite your spouse or partner to spend time with you and your new friends. New relationships often feel a lot less threatening that way—and if your new relationships are affectionate, then your spouse or partner can also observe and learn from the affection you share within them.

Particularly in marriage, it is easy to pin all your hopes, dreams, and expectations on a spouse, even without realizing you have done so. That can be true for a wide variety of needs, including the need for affection. Such expectations are rarely realistic, however, which only sets up your spouse for failure. A better approach is to have reasonable expectations of your spouse and to foster a wider range of affectionate relationships in your life.

Stop and Reflect

We often have unrealistic expectations without realizing it. Before proceeding to Chapter Eleven, consider these questions in relation to your own life:

- When you need or want affection, to whom do you turn? Is it always or almost always to the same person?
- Which of your existing close relationships have the most potential to become more affectionate?
- How is it most comfortable for you to meet new people?

CHAPTER ELEVEN

Strategy #5: Beware of Toxic Affection

Affection has many benefits for individuals and relationships, but that doesn't mean all affection is good. When it comes with strings—instead of being offered freely and unconditionally—affection can have toxic effects on individuals and their relationships. Some people desire affection so much that they accept it in any form . . . and in exchange, they are persuaded to think, say, or do things they wouldn't otherwise agree to. What's worse, many folks in that situation don't realize how others may be taking advantage of them. Wanting more affection in our lives doesn't mean settling for affection that isn't genuine and sincere. Inviting more *genuine* affection requires us—somewhat paradoxically—to turn down offers of affection that burden us with unreasonable or undesirable obligations. To weed out the good from the bad, we have to understand that people can have multiple motives—not all of them positive—when behaving affectionately, and we must be aware of, and resist, toxic forms of affection when we encounter them.

First, Understand the Multiple Motives of Affection

Earlier in the book, I alluded to some of the strange traditions that were common in the church I grew up in. One of those practices is especially relevant here: Whenever prospective new converts were introduced, the existing church members would virtually smother those people with affection. They would say repeatedly how much they love and care about them, and they would shower them with gifts, favors, and other tokens of affection—behaviors that most of us reserve for people we know well. All of this was done to make newcomers feel welcomed and part of the family . . . and it continued unabated as long as they showed interest in joining the church and accepting its beliefs, values, and practices.

Most newcomers seemed to love this outpouring of care, affection, and interest. Indeed, they basked in it. For a variety of reasons, however, many of them eventually decided this wasn't the right church for their needs. The moment they did so, all the love and affection evaporated as quickly as it had materialized. Yesterday, the message was "We love you with all our hearts!" Today, however, it's "We're no longer interested in knowing you."

Over many years, I saw that scene play out dozens of times, maybe even hundreds. One of the many lessons it taught me was that people can have a wide variety of motives for behaving affectionately, and that it's useful to distinguish genuine affection from that which is insincere and manipulative.

Realize That Only Some Affection Is Genuine

It wasn't until many years later, after I became a social scientist, that I discovered the name for this practice of smothering newcomers with affection. It's called *love bombing*, and it is most commonly observed in religious organizations, which use the behavior to attract and retain new members. The practice has been especially widespread in cults, whose beliefs and traditions are often so extreme that newcomers must be duped into joining and committing to them.

Love bombing is a radical example of something that turns out to be relatively common—something I call "toxic affection." If genuine affection is the expression of real love and fondness for someone, then toxic affection is any such expression that has an ulterior motive. Perhaps I say "I love you" because I really do, and I want you to know that. Or, perhaps I say it because there's something I want from you and I think you're more likely to give it to me if I express my love. Children often discover that they can persuade Mom to fork over an extra cookie or an extra few minutes of television time if they tell her how much they love her. (Many moms see right through that sham, of course, but that doesn't mean they fail to acquiesce.) As an adult, though, I may attempt the same trick, telling you how much I love or care for you simply because I need to borrow money, want to sleep with you, or just want you to say the same back to me.

You might think that behavior sounds a bit smarmy, and I would have to agree. Unfortunately, that doesn't mean it's rare.

A few years ago, I surveyed a thousand college undergraduates from around the country to see how common it was to use affection to manipulate or persuade. I asked students if they had ever expressed affection to someone when they didn't really feel it, but had an ulterior motive—and if they had, I asked what their real motive was.

My guess was that more participants than not would say they had used affection in a persuasive or manipulative way, but even I was surprised to find out how frequent the behavior is. Nearly 90 percent reported having expressed affection to someone when they had an ulterior motive—and of those who had, more than half had done so *at least once within the previous month.* This indicated to me that using affection to persuade or manipulate is a relatively ordinary, commonplace act . . . more so than I had first imagined.

When I asked about their reasons for using affection in this way, participants identified a wide variety of motives:

1. We might call some of them *relationship-centered motives,* ones that were meant to enhance the quality or stability of a personal relationship. For instance, some people communicated affection in order to avoid conflict.

2. Others were *recipient-centered motives,* which focused on the needs and desires of the person receiving the affectionate expression. Some people said they showed affection in order to express sympathy or to avoid hurting someone's feelings.

3. Many people in the study, however, expressed *self-centered motives,* or intentions that served the needs and desires of the communicator. Some used affection to elicit money or other resources ("I love you; can you lend me a hundred bucks?"). Others expressed affection as a way of seeking the recipient's forgiveness for a past indiscretion ("I love you; please forgive me for yelling at you yesterday"). And,

as you might imagine, still others used affection to gain sexual access ("I love you; will you sleep with me?").

It may be heartening to know that when people have an ulterior motive for communicating affection, their motive isn't *necessarily* self-serving. Sometimes we express love—even if we aren't really feeling it—because we think that's what the other person needs to hear at the time. However, that's rather like giving someone a false compliment . . . even if it makes the person feel good in the moment, that moment quickly passes, leaving the person with only hollow admiration. And, of course, many manipulative uses of affection *are* for self-serving motives that benefit the sender while disregarding the needs of the recipient.

As interesting as it was to learn how often affection is used in manipulative ways, and for what purposes, the more intriguing question to me is: Why does this strategy work? In other words, why are people persuaded by affectionate expressions that they receive? Let's unravel that mystery next.

Recognize Why Affection Can Be Manipulative

Using something as precious as affection to manipulate others—especially when done for personal gain—may seem distasteful, detestable, or even abhorrent. Often it is. There's a reason why it's so common, though: It works.

By "works," I mean it frequently accomplishes its mission of making the recipient think, feel, believe, or act in the way the sender wants, whether that's in the recipient's best interests or not. Consider nineteen-year-old Angela, a college sophomore who learned that lesson the hard way. She had been seeing her boyfriend (now ex-boyfriend) Ted for just over a month when he pressured her to have sex, something she didn't feel ready for. After hanging out in his apartment one night and having a few too many beers, Ted told Angela that he loved her just as they started kissing and making out. Somewhere in Angela's mind was the thought that he couldn't possibly have fallen in love with her that quickly. In the moment, however, hearing him say it made her feel overwhelmed with joy. She had been waiting to find someone nice to love her, and here he was! She felt so good, in fact, that she ignored her inhibitions and lost her virginity to Ted that evening.

Today, Ted freely admits he didn't really love Angela at all. He wanted sex and he used affection to get it, without considering her needs. He had no intention of building a relationship with Angela, and shortly after that night, he said goodbye and moved on to his next conquest. Angela, however, was left emotionally devastated. She was heartbroken that Ted didn't really love her and angry with herself for believing that he did. Although she eventually built a relationship—and later, a marriage—with someone who genuinely did love her, it took her a long time to trust anyone's expression of affection after her experience with Ted.

Angela is far from the only woman to whom Ted has conveyed love only for the purpose of gaining sexual access. In his experience, it doesn't always work, but it works most of the time. Similarly, the members of my former church used love bombing with every prospective convert, and even though some newcomers didn't choose to stay, many did. Why is this strategy successful?

The answer goes back to an observation I made at the beginning of this book: We humans have a deep and abiding need to belong. We generally reserve affectionate expressions for people we care about, so receiving such an expression makes us feel valued and feeds our drive for inclusion. Because our social needs are so strong, we are willing to help those who (seemingly) feel affection for us. It's a deceptive, manipulative practice to use affection in this way, given that the "affection" isn't genuine and is usually withdrawn if the other person fails to comply with our requests, just as my church members' "affection" evaporated the moment a prospective convert decided not to commit. Nonetheless, using affection in this form can be powerfully persuasive, because of how strongly we want and need to be loved. Few of us relish the thought of rejecting love and attention when others are offering it.

We also feel obliged to help people who love us. That's especially true for our relatives. If you needed a large sum of money or a place to live for several months, whom would you ask? Most people would think of family members first. Now consider the question in a different frame: Whom would you be most likely to help in these ways? I know I would feel a stronger imperative to help, say, my brother than I would to help a non-relative.

That imperative actually has evolutionary roots. Across the history of our species, people who shared more resources with their families than with non-relatives had greater reproductive success, all other things being equal. That's because when I give genetic relatives resources that help them survive and thrive (such as money or shelter), I increase the odds that my own genes will make it into future generations, because those relatives carry my genes. The same isn't true of a friend, neighbor, or coworker—although they may help me in other valuable ways, they don't directly contribute to my genetic success because they don't carry my genes.

All of this creates a unique opportunity for persuasion: If I can make you *think of me as family,* then I can benefit from your evolved tendency to help your family. You might walk right past me on the sidewalk if I said "Can you spare a dime?" for instance, but you'd be more likely to part with your change if I said "Hey brother, can you spare a dime?" Obviously, the thinking part of your brain realizes that I'm not, in fact, your brother . . . but the feeling part of your brain reacts by inclining you to help me as if I were.

Try This

Consider your own motives for conveying affection to others. Think of the last several times you have expressed feelings of love or fondness to someone else, and list your reasons for doing so. What were you trying to accomplish each time? Many of those expressions may have been genuine, of course, but be honest about any that weren't. Were your motives relationship-centered, recipient-centered, or self-centered?

Organizations use this tactic, whether knowingly or not. In many religious groups, for example, much emphasis is placed on the idea that your church is your family. In some churches, it is even commonplace to refer to people using familial terms, such as "Father Emilio" or "Sister Carol." People in such groups may encourage this behavior because it helps them feel closer to each other, but it has the added effect of making it easier to persuade when necessary. We are inclined to help the ones we love, especially family, so to be reminded of their love and connection to us can activate that tendency.

Many people fall victim to these tactics because they're so hungry for affection that they will accept it from anyone, even if it isn't genuine. For those of us who want more affection in our lives, our efforts are hindered rather than helped by this type of manipulative affection. Indeed, it has the toxic effect of duping us into feeling loved while leaving our real need for connection unaddressed. Thus, we do better to identify and avoid such displays, as we'll discuss next.

Second, Learn to Identify and Avoid Toxic Affection

Increasing the amount of genuine affection you have in your life is possible only if you are vigilant about avoiding expressions that burden you with expectations or obligations. One of the worst things about toxic affection, however, is that it is often difficult to notice. Therefore, you'll need to look for the "strings" attached to an expression of affection, and then learn to decline that affection . . . or at least, to accept it cautiously.

Manage Feelings of Obligation

To survive and thrive in our world, humans have evolved a number of specific social tendencies. As I described, one of those is the tendency to help the people who love us, particularly if they are relatives. Another is the propensity to reciprocate favors, or to repay others for the good things they have done for you.

Suppose we're coworkers who meet up for lunch every now and then. If you buy our lunch this week, we will probably both feel it is right and fair that I pay next time. We may deviate from that "my turn-your turn" pattern if we're celebrating a birthday or a promotion, but in general, we both believe it's only fair that we share the burden of paying for the meals we eat together. Consequently, if I skimp on my responsibilities by asking you to pay too many times in a row or "forgetting" my wallet when it's my turn to buy, you would feel taken advantage of and I would feel guilty.

The expectation of tit-for-tat—and the negative emotions we both feel if we violate that expectation—evolved as a way to promote the sharing of resources. In social groups, resources such as money, food, and shelter are finite . . . there's only so much to go around. If you share your resources with me, therefore, it's in your best interests that I do the same for you, instead of benefiting from your generosity while giving you nothing in return. Cheating you may benefit me in the short run, because I would then have more resources to use for myself. It would hurt me in the long run, though, because you (and others who learned from you) would soon stop sharing with me.

The inclination to repay favors therefore promotes the welfare of everyone in the group, making it a beneficial tendency. It's also vulnerable to abuse, just like the tendency to help our families. Earlier I gave the example of someone calling you "Brother" in order to activate your inclination to help your relatives. Similarly, someone can give you a resource, even without your asking for it, simply to make you feel obligated to repay the favor.

Individuals and organizations that want your money use this tactic all the time. Just yesterday, I received in the mail a set of personalized address labels from an animal rights group. Each label features a photo of an animal along with my name and address. They're cute and I'll probably use them, but I never asked for them. They were a gift, and that's the point—by giving me something free of charge, the organization hopes I will feel indebted enough to give something back: a donation. The same principle is at work when you're stopped in traffic and someone starts washing your windshield. You didn't ask them to, but because they did it anyway, you'll feel guilty if you don't offer something in return.

Social relationships work best, that is, when they are equitable. Receiving a resource from someone, even if we didn't request it, makes us feel obligated to give back. In addition to address labels and window-washing services, an expression of affection can be a resource that makes us feel indebted. When someone says "I love you," there's a social expectation that you will reciprocate the gesture. (We become acutely aware of this expectation when we don't feel comfortable saying "I love you too" but we realize that we're supposed to.)

Not everyone who uses affection manipulatively realizes it. At a conscious level, the people in my church weren't *trying* to be persuasive with their affection, nor were they trying to manipulate newcomers to act against their best interests. From their perspective, they were trying to persuade people to act *in their best interests* by joining the group. Nonetheless, their "love" came with strings, which is evident given how quickly it evaporated when newcomers didn't join.

As with any other resource, people can offer affection for the purpose of making others feel indebted. Whether that is done intentionally (as with Ted) or unintentionally (as with my church members), the affection is equally as toxic because it comes with conditions. After identifying toxic expressions of affection, we must then refuse them.

Refuse Toxic Affection

In a book designed to help you get more meaningful connections and affection in your life, the suggestion to refuse affection may seem completely off the mark. Nonetheless, it is good advice, because toxic affection isn't genuine. It deceives you by appearing to be real love, but in truth it is an empty, hollow gesture meant only to manipulate you into thinking, believing, or acting the way the sender wants.

It is difficult to increase real affection in your life if you devote time and attention to insincere, disingenuous expressions of love. What does it mean to refuse those expressions?

Refusing toxic affection doesn't mean rejecting the people who offer it. Rather, it means resolving not to be manipulated by their gestures. Affection works as a persuasive tool because most of us *want it*—after all, we have a strong need for acceptance and inclusion. We are therefore inclined to agree to the requests of people who provide it. A better approach, however, is to make our decisions independently, without allowing affection to be a factor.

That may sound like straightforward advice—but following it isn't easy, for at least two reasons:

1. First, *we want, need, and enjoy affection, so to refuse it goes against our primal motivation to form and nurture close relationships.* Indeed, rejecting expressions of love is difficult, even stressful. That is especially true when the love we are rejecting is genuine, instead of manipulative. Research tells us that unrequited love—which occurs when one person's expression of interest is unreciprocated by the other—is enormously stressful for the person who is rejected. Nota-

bly, however, it is even *more distressing* for the rejecter. It simply goes against our nature to refuse love and affection from others, even if you don't share those feelings. For the same reason, it's not easy to decline even insincere expressions of affection, despite the fact that they may carry unwelcome obligations.

2. The second reason it can be difficult to refuse toxic affection is that *receiving affection makes us feel obliged to reciprocate*, and we're often motivated more by how we feel than by what we think. Take the address labels as an example. By printing and mailing them to me free of charge, the animal rights group did me a favor that I feel some sense of duty to repay. I can certainly override that feeling with rational thought. In this case, I might remind myself that I already contribute money to this group on a monthly basis, which counteracts my sense that I owe them even more for the labels. Arriving at this conclusion, however, required me to set aside my purely emotional response—that is, my feeling that I now owed something to the group—and consider my options in a more rational, emotion-free way.

Remember, refusing toxic affection doesn't mean rejecting people—it means not allowing yourself to be manipulated by their hollow sentiments. That sometimes takes a concerted effort, given that so much of our decision making is driven by emotion. Here are some specific tips:

- Express appreciation for the affection you receive. It won't always be obvious whether others are trying to manipulate you—and even if they are, they may believe their affection is sincere. Unless you know for sure that you're being love bombed, I recommend giving others the benefit of the doubt, such as by saying "thank you, I care for you too" when they offer their affection to you.

- If it's evident that someone is being affectionate only to obligate you to do something, ask yourself whether you would take that action anyway. For instance, Leslie has noticed that her neighbor, Jenna—who serves on the board of the local Red Cross—becomes much friendlier each year during the organization's fundraising drive. Once, Jenna even left Leslie a voicemail message saying, "I hope I can count on my close friends to contribute." Leslie has never felt close to Jenna, so she recognizes this affectionate act for what it is: an attempt to gain a donation. Jenna's false affection aside, however, Leslie supports the work of the Red Cross and would make a donation anyway, so she does.

- When false affection accompanies a request to do something you *wouldn't* otherwise do, consider your options. Even if Leslie didn't feel strongly about the Red Cross, she might have made a token donation in response to Jenna's request simply to keep peace with her neighbor. Otherwise, she might say to Jenna, "I really appreciate the work you do for the Red Cross, but I have other important charities that I support." In this way, Leslie is not rejecting Jenna—in fact, she is complimenting her on her efforts—but she is deciding not to be persuaded by Jenna's insincere affection.

- Suppose you realize you've already acquiesced to the suggestions of people expressing toxic affection—what then? My advice is the same as before: Show gratitude for the affection, but indicate that the priorities for your behavior have changed. Let's say you're a newcomer to my church who has discovered after a period of time that you no longer want to accept its beliefs and practices, but you feel a sense of obligation to please the people who love you. Instead of calling out the congregants for manipulating you, say that you appreciate all the support and affection they have shown you but have decided that your church needs would be best served elsewhere.

In short, refusing toxic affection is about making your own decisions rather than letting others make them for you. Most of us have a strong need to please those who love us, but when the "love" isn't genuine, we can be led—intentionally or not—to act outside our best interests. Therefore, it's better to recognize those situations and adjust our actions accordingly.

Try This

Take a mental inventory of your close relationships, and consider honestly whether the affection you receive in any of them is predicated on your thinking, believing, or acting in a specific manner. If so, develop a healthy skepticism about that affection. You needn't necessarily end those relationships, of course, but it may be best if you don't rely on them to meet your affection needs. Rather, follow the advice of Chapter Ten and nurture relationships that offer you genuine, unconditional affection.

Finally, Separate the Person from the Behavior

When I think about people like Ted, or even the members of my former church, it's easy to feel angry about how they used affection to take advantage of others. Like many, I don't mind being persuaded by logical, well-reasoned arguments, but I feel manipulated and downright used when people try to persuade me with expressions of love. That's all the more true when they do so willingly and knowingly, the way Ted did with Angela. One of the many toxic effects of that behavior is that it erodes my trust in the person.

When this occurs, however, a good lesson is to evaluate the person separately from his or her behavior (at least, as best you can). Unlike Ted, not everyone who uses affection in a persuasive way does so with malicious intent. As we saw in my study of college students, many use affection—even if it's insincere—to benefit the recipient or the relationship instead of themselves. That doesn't excuse the behavior, nor does it mean the "affection" is beneficial instead of toxic. Nonetheless, there is a difference between manipulating others for their own good and doing so only to serve one's own interests, and it's easy to miss this distinction if we simply judge the person based on the behavior alone.

One of the unfortunate things about toxic affection, however, is that it is observed most frequently in those relationships that *should* inspire trust and confidence, such as with loved ones or in a community of worship. Indeed, in my study, the vast majority of people who had used affection persuasively did so within a close personal relationship. Manipulative affection isn't as common in more distant bonds, such as between casual acquaintances, because affection itself isn't as common in those relationships. When it occurs with a close friend or partner, however, that's when it is most difficult—yet most important—to evaluate the person and the behavior separately. The behavior may hurt, and it may even erode some of your trust in that person. Nonetheless, you have a close relationship with him or her for many reasons, and this infraction—especially if it was done to benefit you—needn't necessarily negate the entire relationship. As useful as it is to identify and refuse toxic affection, try to forgive those who use it, especially if your relationships with those people are valuable to you.

Try This

Recall an incident when someone used affection to try to persuade you to think or act in a certain way. In a journal or on your computer, write that person a note explaining how his or her behavior made you feel at the time, and how recalling it makes you feel now. Then, explain why you have chosen to forgive the behavior. It is up to you whether to share your note with the person, but articulating a reason for forgiveness can help you separate the behavior from the person's more positive attributes, and it can also serve as a reminder not to repeat the behavior with other people yourself.

No matter how deprived of affection you feel in your life, you can improve your situation only by inviting sincere, genuine affection. Unfortunately, some forms of affection are manipulative, leading you to think or act in certain ways as a condition of the affection. Such expressions have toxic effects on individuals and relationships, and are never a substitute for the genuine love and connection we need.

Stop and Reflect

Toxic affection is harmful, yet surprisingly common. Before going forward to Chapter Twelve, think about these queries as they relate to toxic affection in your own life:

- Among your close friends and relatives, whom do you think is most likely to use affection in a manipulative way? What leads you to that conclusion?
- Can you recall ever expressing affection when you didn't really feel it, but with some other purpose in mind? What was your motive?
- In what ways can you protect yourself from being persuaded by toxic affection in the future?

CHAPTER TWELVE

Strategy #6: Be Optimistic But Realistic

Over the last several chapters, we have explored a range of strategies for inviting genuine affection in your life and for capitalizing on the affection you already receive. As I've pointed out, not every tactic will work equally well for every person—rather, each of us needs to consider which approaches are most appropriate, and most likely to be successful, given our individual life circumstances.

Regardless of which strategies we employ, however, it is useful to craft expectations for ourselves and others that are both optimistic and realistic. That's not always easy. When trying to enact change in their lives, many people become frustrated when improvements don't come about as quickly or as fully as they hope. Frustration can easily give way to pessimism, the belief that things will never get better. When people become pessimistic, they stop trying, because they figure it makes no difference what they do. To achieve real change, therefore, it makes sense to avoid that trap and remain as optimistic as possible.

Having optimism doesn't mean living in a fantasy world, though. As important as it is to stay positive, it is equally important to have expectations that are realistic. You can attract more affection in your life—but that may not happen in the way you expect, nor as quickly as you might want. Even as you're optimistic, therefore, it pays to keep a realistic watch on your progress.

For all these reasons, I have chosen to end this book with the only strategy that I think is relevant across the board, no matter what your circumstances. As I'll explain, being optimistic but realistic requires you to acknowledge that your relationships have a natural ebb and flow, and to choose to work *with* that rather than *against* it. It also calls for you to be understanding and patient with those around you, and to ask for help whenever necessary. Finally, when optimism and realism clash, I recommend favoring realism by recognizing when a given relationship has run its course.

First, Honor the Ebb and Flow of Relationships

Being in a long-term relationship is a bit like riding ocean waves. Sometimes relationships move along smoothly, with much affection and little conflict, and sometimes even the smallest achievements feel like a struggle. It's easy to get caught in the belief that healthy relationships always involve smooth sailing—but buying into that belief causes people to overreact whenever they face waves.

To keep your expectations realistic, therefore, it's useful to remember that relational ebbs and flows are normal and not something to be feared. Let's examine how you can approach change and development in your relationships sensibly rather than unrealistically.

Accept That Relationships Involve Tension

Anyone who's been part of a pair—whether romantic or not—knows that people go back and forth over time in terms of what they want. Today they long to be close to you, but tomorrow they'll want their space. Yesterday they felt like being spontaneous, but now they prefer the certainty of a schedule. When people waver this way, it can seem to outsiders as though they can't make up their minds about what they want or need. If you're in a long-term relationship, though, you know that these conflicts are entirely normal.

In fact, they have a name: Scientists call them *dialectical tensions*. According to research, dialectical tensions occur in a relationship when people feel torn between two opposing but equally necessary desires. In her marriage, for example, Kelly wants to be intimately connected to her husband Jeff, but she also wants to have her own identity and be able to make decisions for herself. She desires *connectedness*, in other words, but she also desires its opposite, *autonomy*. These are opposing forces: By definition, the more connectedness someone experiences, the less autonomy he or she has, and vice versa. Yet Kelly wants both of these in her relationship, as many of us do.

Other dialectical tensions are also common. For instance, many people also waver between wanting their relationships to be dependable and certain (i.e., to have *predictability*) and enjoying a few surprises now and then (i.e., to have *novelty*). Many of us also enjoy sharing and self-disclosure (to have *openness*), yet we also prefer to keep a few secrets of our own (to have *closedness*).

These types of tensions are normal, and by themselves they're no cause for concern. To have realistic expectations about affection in your relationship, though, it's necessary to factor them in. Even if you seek more affection in your life, that probably isn't the only thing you need or desire, nor do you want it all the time. The same is almost certainly true of your spouse or partner. Intimacy, connectedness, and affection are important in close relationships, but so are moments of solitude and autonomy.

As you work toward attracting greater affection from your loved ones, focus on balancing your expectations by making room for the tensions that permeate most close relationships. When a partner communicates affectionately with you, appreciate and enjoy that behavior in the moment. That's what Corinne, aged fifty-four, tries to do. Married at age twenty-one and widowed before she turned forty, Corinne has spent the last several years feeling deeply affection deprived. She started dating Joe, aged fifty-nine, almost two years ago—and like most relationships, theirs is characterized by an ongoing tension between craving intimacy and appreciating the interests they pursue separately.

Because she understands and accepts that tension as normal, Corinne is able to value Joe's expressions of affection without devaluing the independence that they also both enjoy. She's happy when he grabs her in an impromptu embrace in the kitchen or when he plays the piano because he knows she loves hearing the music. More important, she has learned to appreciate these experiences in the moment, without expecting Joe to be affectionate with her during every waking hour or to give up the hobbies he enjoys pursuing on his own.

Joe's a naturally affectionate guy, but if your own loved ones are stretching their normal bounds of behavior in order to show more affection, it is especially important to remain patient, appreciate the affection you receive, and offer them the space to provide it without feeling as though they're giving away their independence by doing so. In truth, it's also important to give yourself space in which to receive, absorb, and appreciate the affection they are providing you now, instead of focusing on how much more is to come.

Be Prepared for Intensity to Wax and Wane

On that note, remember that affectionate communication is a behavior, not a permanent state of being. Even partners who share intensely passionate or intimate affection with each other do so only for discrete periods, not constantly. Most emotional experiences cannot be sustained at a high level of intensity for very long at a time—they simply require too much physical and psychological energy. After going through an episode of intense anger, for instance, we cool down and return to a state of normalcy. Even if our anger festers, it does so at a more manageable level of intensity, because few of us have the energy to sustain extreme anger for too long. The same is true for most emotional experiences, and that includes feeling and expressing affection.

Most people find it more common—and much more manageable—for affectionate behavior to wax and wane over time. Partners Blake and Taylor have certainly found that to be true in their relationship, for example. Together for nearly four years, they have come to appreciate that episodes of intense affection—whether it's having sex, holding hands on the couch, or talking about their feelings for each other—are interspersed with many other, more mundane experiences, such as planning a shopping list, bathing their German Shepherd, and watching the evening news. Although they both love and crave their moments of affection, they realize those episodes are temporal.

More important, they recognize that moments of affection are meaningful *precisely because* they are intermittent instead of constant. Feelings of affection can smolder for a prolonged period (just as anger can fester), and they often do so in long-term, significant relationships. Nonetheless, the mundane, day-to-day experiences are necessary so that you can appreciate the more intense affectionate experiences.

Try This

Over the course of a normal day in your marriage or your most important relationship, be aware of the waxing and waning of various emotions. Note the times when you feel affectionate toward the other person, and be equally aware of those moments when other emotions—or no emotions—compete for attention. At the end of the day, reflect on the ebbs and flows you experienced within your relationship, and even if you are ultimately seeking more affection from the other person, take a moment to feel gratitude for the affection you were able to share.

What qualifies as "intense" depends, of course, on your experience and your own orientation to affection. A hug and kiss seem run-of-the-mill to Blake and Taylor, for example, because they commonly show their love for each other in these ways. In Blake's relationship with his father, however, he considers a hug to be a substantial and intense expression of affection. That's because his dad isn't nearly as demonstrative as he is. Although Blake always receives a firm handshake from his father, he recalls his dad hugging him only during significant life events, such as his wedding and his graduation from college. Those hugs therefore seem more intense and notable than the ones he receives daily from Taylor, both because they're less frequent and because Blake knows his dad isn't especially comfortable being affectionate in that way. As we think about the intensity of affection varying over time, then, it is useful to keep in mind that each relationship has its own barometer.

That affection waxes and wanes may seem obvious, but we can easily be blinded to the obvious when considering what we want from others. It's easy to over-romanticize close relationships, expecting them to provide intense and nonstop intimacy and judging them deficient when they don't. No matter how much you want affection from your loved ones, you set them up for failure when you pitch your expectations at an unreasonably high level. If you accept that even intense affection will wax and wane over time, then you can learn to appreciate its peaks and not worry about its valleys.

Second, Be Understanding

We have seen in this book that a wide variety of factors lead people to be less affectionate than you want:

- Some don't grow up with families that positively reinforce affectionate behavior.
- Some find showing affection to be risky or scary.

- Others have had bad experiences with communicating affection in previous relationships.
- Still others simply aren't genetically predisposed to behave affectionately.

No matter the reasons, whenever you ask someone to be more affectionate with you, you are asking that person to change. It therefore pays to be understanding by remembering that change is often difficult and that help is available.

Remember That Change Is Difficult

You might have heard the phrase, "The only constant in life is change." There's certainly truth to that statement. When people say that, though, they're usually referring to change that happens *despite our best-laid plans*, such as unforeseen developments in our relationships, our careers, or our health. They usually aren't talking about the kind of change we want, as when we try to eat more sensibly, exercise more frequently, or save more money. Intentional change is difficult—which is why, for many of us, our New Year's resolutions go to seed before the end of January.

Unintentional change happens to us continuously, in other words, but that doesn't mean it's easy to enact intentional, positive change in our lives. Those fortunate souls who never have trouble working out more or spending less are few and far between. For the rest of us, bringing about positive change is a challenge . . . and sustaining it in the long term is even tougher.

That's all the more true when your efforts at change are directed at someone else. It's hard enough to make yourself adopt healthier habits. In comparison, getting others to change often feels like a Herculean task. Anyone who has tried getting a partner to be more affectionate knows how true that is. Although any type of progress—even in personal relationships—ultimately requires change and growth, bringing about the changes you desire in someone else is often a major struggle.

As you implement various strategies for inviting affection, including those described in this book, it is therefore manifestly important to remain patient. Specifically:

- *Don't expect change to happen on your schedule.* When Marian determined that she wanted her boyfriend Travis to show her more affection, she decided to be proactive about making that happen. Her efforts were well conceived, in that she invited affection from Travis instead of demanding it and she modeled the forms of affection she hoped to receive. She even recognized some previously unacknowledged forms of affection he was already providing. Even as she made smart choices, Marian expected her efforts to produce immediate change, and she was therefore disheartened when Travis didn't become more affectionate according to her timetable. When encouraging change and growth in others, you must realize that *imagining what you want someone else to be* is easier than *becoming that person.* Much as you may hope for quick solutions to affection deprivation (or any relationship issue), the reality is that people change when *they* are ready, not just when *you* are ready.

- *Recognize the other person's efforts.* I pointed out earlier that it helps to acknowledge and show gratitude for the effort your partner makes to show you more affection. When people try to adopt new behaviors, new skills, or new ways of being—and when their efforts are rewarded with favorable feedback and attention—their changes are positively reinforced. Decades of research have shown positive reinforcement to be one of the most effective methods of bringing about behavioral change in others. Being optimistic about attracting more affection means believing that you can succeed, and positively reinforcing the expressions of affection you desire is an effective and meaningful way to contribute to your success.

- *Try not to blame.* Whenever you invite someone to change— even if it's to increase affection—you are at least implicitly suggesting that there's something wrong or undesirable about the person right now. After all, you don't ask for more affection when you already get enough. Despite that implication, however, blaming the person for not being more affectionate is seldom constructive. As we've explored, there's a multitude of reasons why some of us are less affectionate than others. Rather than blaming your partner for not meeting your expectations already, keep your focus on the positive changes you want to encourage.

- *Stay patient with yourself, as well.* As useful as it is to exercise patience with others, it is equally helpful to remain patient with yourself. In a close relationship, one person's changes affect both people, so if your partner is working to become more affectionate, his or her efforts have an effect on you as well. Remember that even positive change can take a toll on your energy, so remain patient as you both adjust to a more affectionate way of interacting with each other.

Ask for Help When Needed

As we've observed, change is difficult enough when we're focused on our own behaviors; it's even more challenging when we try to change the behaviors of someone else. Calling these goals difficult doesn't mean they're impossible, of course, but it does mean that our efforts can benefit from help along the way. Besides recognizing that change is hard, part of being understanding is also being willing to ask for help when you need it.

Lean on a Friend

Recall Corinne, whose story we encountered earlier in this chapter. In her boyfriend Joe, she has found an affectionate partner and lover. They enjoy the time they spend together, while also allowing each other time to pursue individual interests. It's a great relationship for both of them—but it didn't start out that way. When they first began dating, Joe spent most of his free time working on his hobbies, whether tinkering on cars all day in the garage, going pheasant hunting with his buddies, or getting lost in a good book. He valued the fact that Corinne understood his need to pursue his own interests, yet at the start of their relationship, he was overlooking her needs for affection in the process. It took effort on Corinne's part to encourage him to be more affectionate—and like many people in that situation, Corinne became frustrated when Joe didn't catch on as quickly as she wanted.

That's when she reached out to her close friend Gayla for help. Gayla was a longtime friend from church who was like a sister to Corinne. And, she was no stranger to the problems Corinne was experiencing, having gone through something similar with her husband Charlie.

As they spent time talking, Gayla helped Corinne to see that she may have been too subtle in her attempts to invite more affection from Joe. Joe cannot read her mind, she pointed out, and despite being a loving guy, he's not particularly sensitive to subtle hints and cues. Through these conversations, Corinne came to realize that she had, in fact, been expecting Joe to know what she wanted and needed on his own, without being informed, and she now understood that it would help to be a bit more direct in expressing her desires. That doesn't mean demanding affection, just inviting it in a more perceptible, less subtle way.

Corinne benefited by reaching out to Gayla for help, not only because Gayla had been through a similar struggle, but also because she helped Corinne to see her own situation in a new light. It is difficult to see the forest when we're chained to a tree. In other words, it's hard to view your problems from any perspective other than your own—as a result, you can fail to recognize factors that are impeding your progress, just as Corinne didn't realize her invitations for affection were too subtle for Joe's sensitivity level. It took a third party, one who was uninvolved in the problem itself (Gayla), to help her see what she was missing.

Consider a Counselor

Many of us are blessed with good friends who can help us the way Gayla helped Corinne. For a variety of reasons, though, it sometimes makes sense to talk with a professional counselor for support. For one, your good friends may not be close by or easily accessible. Even if they are, there may be aspects of your relationship that you don't feel comfortable sharing with them. Finally, even though your friends may be able to see the situation more clearly than you can, they may also be unsure of how to advise you. Especially if they are friends with your spouse or partner as well, they may even end up feeling caught in the middle, which is always an uncomfortable spot in which to put a friend.

In contrast, a professional counselor (PC) or a marriage and family therapist (MFT) is trained to help. They can listen in ways that are supportive and empathic but that are also directed at helping you construct a plan for resolution. They can teach you to talk more openly with your loved ones, and they can point out and help you correct mistakes you may not be aware that you're making.

Our personal friends can be immensely helpful, but their advice may reflect only what has worked for them in the past, which may or may not be relevant to your circumstances. PCs and MFTs, on the other hand, can consider your situation in a broader context and advise you on what generally works, rather than describing only what has worked in their own lives. Between your friends and the professionals available to you, it pays to reach out for help when you need it.

Try This

Another person's efforts at change are easier to appreciate when you recognize that person's barriers to change. Based on your knowledge of your spouse or partner, take note of what usually inhibits his or her affectionate behavior. As you notice expressions of affection, praise the person's behaviors while acknowledging the effort they required. If you know your partner is shy about expressing affection in public, but he kisses you in a public setting anyway, you could tell him how happy that made you feel and how much you appreciate it, especially because you know it wasn't easy for him to do. That statement conveys the message that you value the gesture and helps your partner feel understood.

Finally, Consider Moving on If All Else Fails

For the most part, optimism and realism work nicely in tandem. As we've seen, keeping your expectations optimistic but realistic is a good strategy, as it helps you remain understanding and patient and avoid discouragement. Reality sometimes makes it difficult to stay optimistic, however, such as when it becomes evident that a particular relationship has run its course and is probably not salvageable.

That happens. Despite sentiments such as "'til death do us part," many marriages and significant partnerships—even friendships—have a finite lifespan. Most of us have gone through at least one breakup. When the warning signs appear that a relationship is headed for dissolution, you must decide whether to cling to a false sense of optimism or take a realistic position and accept that the relationship is over.

Being realistic about a relationship's end is often difficult, especially for people who feel deprived of affection already. If you haven't cultivated a broader range of affectionate relationships in your life, letting go of the one person from whom you desperately want affection can seem impossible. In that instance, it's easy to let optimism trump realism and fall into a state of denial.

If a relationship is, in fact, salvageable, then it makes sense to invest time and energy toward saving it, assuming you want to stay in it. Indeed, many couples go through months or even years of counseling for that very reason, often with positive results. I'm certainly not advocating jumping ship on a relationship just because there's turbulence. What I am saying is that if the relationship has truly come to its conclusion, then continuing to seek affection from that partner is fruitless. People take that approach when they're in denial . . . but a better approach is to let realism win over hollow optimism and be willing to move on. There is much affection in the world, and each of us deserves his or her share. Seeking love from a sinking relationship wastes your efforts and keeps you from enjoying the true affection that awaits you.

Try This

Any relationship—whether romantic or not—can reach a natural ending point. If you find yourself in a friendship or romantic relationship that appears to be a lost cause, reflect honestly on your willingness and readiness to move on. As you do, make a mental list of others in your life—such as family members or other friends—with whom you can nurture more affectionate relationships in the process. Although difficult, the end of one treasured relationship can spark renewed love and affection in another. We just have to be willing to let it.

Having optimism means believing your situation can improve, and being realistic means recognizing that improvement takes time and isn't always feasible. Seeking change in a partner benefits from a healthy dose of both. No matter which other strategies you use to invite affection, remaining optimistic yet realistic offers you the best chance for success.

Stop and Reflect

As we approach the end of our journey together in this book, take a moment to reflect on the following questions:

- Which of the strategies we have explored in Part Three make you the most optimistic? Which seem most realistic?
- How do you remain patient while encouraging change in others?
- In what ways will you address affection hunger in your own life?

The End of Loneliness

It was a dark point in his life when Juan Mann felt so hungry for social connection that he literally took to the streets to share a hug with anyone who was willing. Although few of us would take such a dramatic measure, millions upon millions of us can identify with the loneliness and affection hunger that he experienced, because we feel it too. Affection is far more than a luxury for our highly social species—it's a genuine need, one that so many of us fall short of meeting. Even if we don't stand on a street corner giving out hugs, our affection hunger may encourage us to eat too much, gamble excessively, meet up with strangers we encounter online, or accept affection that comes with unwanted obligations, all in an effort to fill the void that loneliness represents.

As we've seen, though, there's much hope for those of us who find ourselves craving attention and affection. Even though every strategy won't be equally applicable to every person's life circumstances, each offers a clear take-home message for thinking about and battling affection hunger, and I encourage you to consider how every strategy can be useful in your own life.

Affection hunger doesn't usually appear overnight, so we can't expect any strategy to eliminate it overnight. With effort, optimism, and a bit of time, however, each of us can build for ourselves the genuine relationships for which we hunger. Remember that loneliness isn't necessarily about being alone—it's about missing the significant connections to our friends, families, and romantic partners that feed our deep and abiding need to belong. As we work to build, nurture, and maintain those meaningful bonds, we can truly find within our grasp the loneliness cure.

For Further Reading

The material in this book represents decades of research by other social scientists and me. For those who want a more in-depth treatment of certain topics, I recommend the following sources:

Baumeister, R.F., and Leary, M.R. (1995). The need to belong: Desire for interpersonal attachments as a fundamental human motivation. *Psychological Bulletin* 117: 497–529.

Cacioppo, J.T., and Patrick, W. (2008). *Loneliness: Human nature and the need for social connection.* New York, NY: W.W. Norton.

Floyd, K. (2006). *Communicating affection: Interpersonal behavior and social context.* Cambridge, England: Cambridge University Press.

Floyd, K. (2014). Relational and health correlates of affection deprivation. *Western Journal of Communication* 78: 383–403.

Harlow, H.F. (1958). The nature of love. *American Psychologist* 13: 673–685.

House, J.S., Landis, K.R., and Umberson, D. (1988). Social relationships and health. *Science* 241: 540–545.

About the Author

PHOTO BY LYN SIMS

KORY FLOYD is a professor of family and interpersonal communication at Arizona State University. He has studied the communication of affection in close relationships and its connection with health and wellness for more than twenty years. Dr. Floyd's work has been featured on the *Today* show, HuffPost Live, NPR and BBC radio, and in articles in dozens of magazines and newspapers, including *Women's Health*, *Redbook*, *Glamour*, *Seattle Times*, *Denver Times*, and *Cleveland Plain Dealer*. He has written multiple textbooks and scholarly books about communication in personal relationships, and he writes the *Affectionado* blog for *Psychology Today*. He currently lives in Tucson, Arizona.